smartfoods
for tweens

Anna Jacob & Ng Hooi Lin

Marshall Cavendish
Editions

Editor: Lydia Leong
Designer: Rachel Chen Choon Jet
Photographer: Joshua Tan, Elements by the Box

Published by Marshall Cavendish Cuisine
An imprint of Marshall Cavendish International
1 New Industrial Road, Singapore 536196

Other Marshall Cavendish Offices:
Marshall Cavendish Ltd.5th Floor, 32–38 Saffron Hill, London EC1N 8FH • Marshall
Cavendish Corporation. 99 White Plains Road, Tarrytown NY 10591-9001, USA •
Marshall Cavendish International (Thailand) Co Ltd. 253 Asoke, 12th Flr, Sukhumvit
21 Road, Klongtoey Nua, Wattana, Bangkok 10110, Thailand • Marshall Cavendish
(Malaysia) Sdn Bhd, Times Subang, Lot 46, Subang Hi-Tech Industrial Park,
Batu Tiga, 40000 Shah Alam, Selangor Darul Ehsan, Malaysia

Marshall Cavendish is a trademark of Times Publishing Limited

National Library Board Singapore Cataloguing in Publication Data

Jacob, Anna, 1962-
Smart foods for tweens / Anna Jacob and Ng Hooi Lin. – Singapore : Marshall
Cavendish Editions, c2009.
p. cm.
ISBN-13 : 978-981-261-597-8
ISBN-10 : 981-261-597-0

1. Cookery. 2. Children – Nutrition. I. Ng, Hooi Lin. II. Title.

TX714
641.5622 -- dc22   OCN244458191

Printed in Singapore by KWF Printing Pte Ltd

Give your children a headstart
in life! Nourish them well
to maximise their genetic
potential for physical and
mental growth!

contents

Acknowledgements

We would like to thank all the wonderful people who made this book possible.

Lydia Leong, our editor. Thank you for believing in us and giving us this great opportunity to celebrate our appreciation of wholesome foods, and to give of our best to the young ones around us.

Rachel Chen, our designer, for taking our words, work and dreams and making them a visual delight, page after page.

Joshua Tan, our food photographer. You make every food item and dish a work of art. Thank you for expressing our thoughts so beautifully through the lens.

Ezra Kan, Jaclyn Phua, Jordan Goh, Katelyn Phua, Muhd Izzat, Petchara Newson, Ryan Phua, Stephanie Yuen and **Thomas Abraham** for simply having fun and being yourselves during the photo shoot. Special thanks also to the parents who took time out to be with their children.

The Lord Jesus. I can do nothing except that You bless, guide and support me.

My husband, **Jibby Jacob**, for the space and support you give me for every creative endeavour. I cannot begin to express my love and gratitude.

My daughter, **Divya Susan Jacob**. You truly are my inspiration to reach for the stars.

My mother, **Elizabeth Abraham**. You are my anchor through the ups and downs of life.

Ng Hooi Lin. You have been a great colleague and an inspiring friend.

Myrna Partible. Thank you for allowing us to mess up the kitchen day after day.

~ Anna Jacob

My mother, **Koh Koon Qui** and my sisters, **Hooi Chueen** and **Yuen Choo**, for filling my life with so much love and joy. **Anna Jacob**, for inviting me to work on this book.

My good friends, **Wong Chen Siang, Christina Ng, Ng Boon Huat, Chang Wei Fung** and **Zhang Qinghua**, for being an important part of my life, inspiring and supporting me all the time.

My blog readers, for your support and encouragement.

Myrna Partible, for teaching me to cook from scratch.

~ Ng Hooi Lin

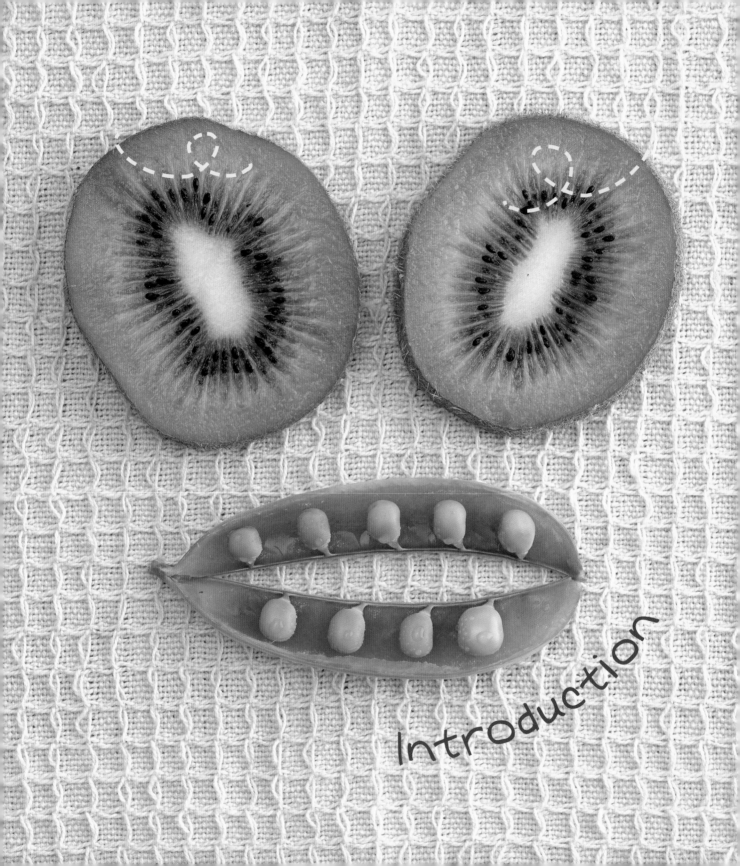

Introduction

Healthy and well-nourished children have the best chance to live life well. Optimal nourishment throughout childhood ensures that they will get to maximise their genetic potential for physical and mental growth.

Children between the ages of six and 12, or 'tweens', as we call them, have strong food preferences and quite a defined personal eating style. The pressures of the school schedule, extra-curricular activities, child care arrangements, peer opinions and food marketing will influence your children's food choices and eating patterns. While you have less control now over your children's food choices than when they were babies or toddlers, you are still the ultimate gatekeeper of your children's diet. Whenever you can, make every food choice count for more nourishment.

Smart Foods for Tweens brings you over 70 quick and easy, yet wholesome and delicious recipes that feature nutrient-dense food ingredients. Trust us; you do not have to go to a cooking class to learn to prepare these dishes. Go ahead, put on your apron and start whipping up smart food choices today. The dishes are good not only for tweens, but for everyone else in the family too!

Bon Appétit!

Anna Jacob & Ng Hooi Lin

Understanding Your Tween-ager

Tweens Grow
Between the ages of six and 12, children continue to grow, but not as rapidly as they did when they were babies and toddlers. Growth patterns of tweens vary. Some grow slowly and steadily throughout these years, shooting up only after they reach their teens. Others grow rapidly during this period, but do not experience a dramatic growth spurt in adolescence.

Tweens Mature into Adolescents
Puberty sets in between the middle and late stages of the tween phase, and girls tend to mature earlier than boys. During this time, children experience physical changes that slowly but surely transform them into adults. Parents need to be aware of these changes and be sensitive and supportive of their children's physical and emotional needs at this time.

Tweens Experience Social and Emotional Change
Entering school and interacting with peers and teachers, slowly wean tweens off their dependence on parents and caregivers. Children begin to develop their personalities and preferences.

As your children begin to exert independence, you will need to be discrete in providing support, while setting clear boundaries for safe and acceptable behaviours.

Nourishing Tweens

Good nutrition fuels the rapid growth and development that occurs in tween-hood. Tweens need a balanced diet that provides them with sufficient nutrients for optimal nourishment. (Refer to the table, Dietary Reference Intake (DRI) for Tweens, page 164 for more detail). Aim to achieve these goals with an array of wholesome foods.

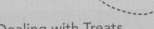

Dealing with Treats

Many delicious, but not necessarily nutritious foods and drinks are readily available to your children. It is not realistic to prevent them from consuming these foods and drinks completely, but here is a simple guide to help you help your tweens manage these treats.

Deep-fried, oily and high-fat foods
- Limit intake of such foods to no more than twice a week.
- Keep the portion small e.g. just one chicken wing or half a cup of potato chips or crisps.

Sweetened foods and drinks
- Limit intake of such foods to no more than 9–11 teaspoonfuls of sugar a day.
- Read food labels or log on to public nutrition databases to estimate the sugar content of popular foods.

Tween Feeding Challenges

Personal Preferences
Your children may now clearly express preference and dislike for specific foods and have their personal eating styles. While being flexible to a point, guide your tweens to develop healthy relationships with food and eating.

Weight Issues
The rising prevalence of obesity in children is due to a lifestyle that supports overeating, indulgence in high-energy foods and sedentary activities. Despite being overweight, many children are undernourished as they tend to consume foods and drinks that are high in energy but low in nutrients.

On the other hand, some tweens also struggle with eating enough. Fear of gaining weight, societal pressures and the need for control are some triggers that cause under eating. But eating too little will curtail the achievement of growth potential.

Feeding Skills
Let your children master the skills of self-feeding. Allow them to participate in and take some responsibility for menu decisions, shopping and serving food. This will go a long way towards helping them inculcate healthy attitudes about food and eating.

Peer Pressure
Friends have a great influence on your children's diet. Do not be surprised if your children begin to indulge in candies and fried foods that you have made only as an occasional treat. Take time to talk to your children about the foods and drinks they consume at school. Set limits on how much and how often treats should be consumed. On the other hand, tweens may also be introduced to a variety of healthier foods or foods from other cultures by watching what their friends eat.

Provide your tweens with a wide variety of food every day to help them appreciate the different tastes and textures.

Media Influences

Tweens will be exposed to food marketing. The food industry uses television, radio and print advertisements, information brochures, Internet games, sponsorship of competitions and many other ways to get children to consume their products. You cannot entirely protect your children from these influences, but you can guide them on how much and how often these foods should be consumed, so that overall, their diet remains healthy and well-balanced.

Why Should You Take Charge?

Food habits inculcated in childhood will carry on into adolescence and adulthood. Poor nutrition puts children at risk of developing chronic lifestyle diseases such as heart disease, diabetes, certain cancers and even osteoporosis, later on in life. Parents can set the stage for better health, so be well informed about good nutrition and stay involved in your children's eating habits.

Choosing Smart Foods

We eat to stay alive, but eating too little or too much does not support optimal health. To stay well nourished, the foods we choose to eat need to deliver at least 36 essential nutrients each day! Add on to that list thousands of other beneficial compounds, called phytonutrients, found naturally in food and, you will begin to appreciate how complex staying well nourished really is!

Thankfully, nature packages these wonderful nutrients and beneficial phytonutrients in wholesome foods, which we call Smart Foods! Note that while we appreciate the special nutritional contribution of a particular food, no one food can provide all the nutrients we need. So, a fundamental tenet of good nutrition is to eat a wide variety of wholesome foods.

Tips to Feed Your Tween Right

- Offer a variety of food to help your children learn to appreciate a wide variety of tastes and flavours.

- Provide a well-balanced diet each day.

- Limit foods with added sugar, sodium-containing seasonings and fat, especially saturated and trans fats.

- Establish a regular pattern of meals and healthy snacks to keep your children well nourished.

- Ensure that your children eat breakfast every day.

Nutritionists provide guidance on how much of each of the 36 nutrients we need each day. Tabulated as the Dietary Reference Intake (DRI), this consensus of the best scientific evidence to date, provides nutrient goals to aim for each day. Looking at the numbers will make you dizzy, so a simple way to achieve the goals is to follow the Healthy Diet Pyramid, a food selection guide promoted by national health authorities, which features four basic food groups — grains, vegetables fruit and protein-rich foods. By including foods from these four food groups in the right portions, you are set to achieve almost all the nutrient goals.

All natural foods provide valuable nutrients and natural plant compounds called phytonutrients. Some are, however, a better source of particular nutrients or phytonutrients than others. With this book, we aim to make each mouthful count for more nourishment and deliver more nutrients for every calorie your children consume. Here is how it works.

Make each mouthful count for more nourishment with nutrient-dense foods.

The Smart Foods Guidance System
To help us pick the best foods to feature in this book, we compared the nutrient content of foods that are easily available in local markets and supermarkets against the nutrient goals for each day. With the results, we ranked them to create our list of Smart Foods for every food group — grains, fruit, vegetables, dairy products, meat, beans, nuts and seeds. Featuring these nutrient-dense chart toppers in your children's diet more often will help them achieve their daily nutrient goals with greater ease.

Read on to learn more about the star nutrients and phytonutrients in each of the Smart Foods, then talk to your children about the goodness of the foods they eat. You will soon transform them into nutrition ambassadors!

The Smart Foods Recipes

We can write and provide recipes for Smart Foods, but there will be little benefit unless they are prepared and consumed. Thus, we have kept the recipes quick and easy for the convenience of parents and caregivers, and delicious to entice tweens.

We have also tried to keep the recipes as low in fat, sugar and sodium (from salt and sodium-containing sauces) as possible to keep the final dish nutritious, but tasty. Train your children to accept the milder flavours, and over time, they will appreciate wholesome foods.

These recipes for Smart Foods are categorised as beverages, snacks, soups, main meals, sides and desserts to help you plan nutritious menus for your family. Each recipe serves a family of four — two adults and two children. Adapt them as necessary to suit the needs of your family.

The cooking methods are simple and carefully selected to optimise the nutritional value of the main ingredient featured. Read the recipes carefully, then measure out and prepare the ingredients before you start cooking. You do not have to be a chef to whip up these recipes. That's a promise!

Invite your tweens to help you prepare and even cook some of the dishes. The more savvy they are about wholesome food and healthy cooking, the more likely they are to stay well nourished through life. So go ahead, make Smart Foods a family affair today!

Icons Explained
Use the handy icons above each recipe to manage your time well. If you are in a hurry, choose recipes that can be cooked up quickly. When you have more time on hand, try out the recipes that take a bit longer.

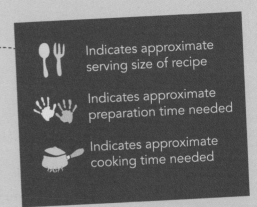

Indicates approximate serving size of recipe

Indicates approximate preparation time needed

Indicates approximate cooking time needed

Star Nutrients Explained

We have highlighted which nutrients are plentiful in each recipe, and listed them under three categories. This is the breakdown:

Source:	17%–25% of DRI
Good Source:	more than 25%–50% of DRI
Excellent Source:	more than 50% of DRI

Nutritional Analysis Explained

The nutrients highlighted in the Nutritional Analysis table are of particular importance for the maintenance of good health and the prevention of disease. The values declared are a close approximation of the nutrient content per serving. Here's how you can use the information well.

- If you are concerned about the intake of a particular nutrient, e.g. calcium, select recipes that are higher in calcium by checking the Nutritional Analysis table.

- Compare the values per serve to the DRI on page 164 to check out its contribution to your children's overall diet.

Smart Foods Menu Planning

The Smart Foods meal planner (page 30) aims to provide sample menus for your family. But first, here's a lowdown on the principles of healthy menu planning, so you can whip up creative meal plans of your own!

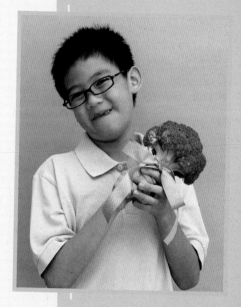

Do not despair if your children reject vegetables. Keep offering them an interesting variety of vegetables every day, and they will soon learn to accept and enjoy them.

Great Grains

Cereal grains have been the staple of Asian diets for thousands of years. Traditional choices include rice, noodles and breads such as *man tou*, idli and chapatti. With the globalisation of food cultures, Western bread, buns, cereal, pasta and biscuits also feature regularly in Asian family menus today.

Nutrient Power

Grains are great sources of carbohydrates that provide fuel for the body to support physical and mental activities. Every grain is made up of four distinct parts: husk, bran, endosperm and germ. Until the introduction of milling, people ate the grains 'whole', with the bran, endosperm and germ intact. Modern diets however, commonly feature 'refined' grains, such as white rice, refined breakfast cereals and refined flours that are used to produce white bread, cakes, biscuits, noodles and pasta.

While refined grains remain a good source of carbohydrates, whole grains naturally have more vitamins, minerals, fibre and phytonutrients. In fact, whole grains are a unique package of nutrients that work together to promote health and prevent certain diseases such as diabetes, cardiovascular disease and some cancers.

Healthier Choices

- Choose whole grains like oats, brown rice, wholemeal flour, barley and kernel corn.
- If you buy packaged foods, read ingredient labels to look for products that list whole grains among the first few ingredients.
- Ideally, whole grain products should contain at least 2 g fibre per serving and be low in fat and sugar.

Portion Ration

Aim for five to six servings of grain foods each day — five servings for physically smaller and less active kids, and six for the taller and more active ones. One serving of grain food is defined as two slices of bread, half a bowl of cooked rice or noodles or four plain biscuits.

Choices of Great Grains

- Whole wheat products
- Brown rice
- Corn kernels
- Oats
- Barley

Star Nutrients in Wholegrains

Vitamins	Minerals	Fibre	Phytonutrients
Vitamin E	Iron	Insoluble	Flavonoids
Thiamin (B_1)	Phosphorus	Soluble	Lignans
Riboflavin (B_2)	Magnesium		Phytosterols
Niacin (B_3)	Selenium		
	Zinc		

Vital Veggies

Vegetables, with their unique colours, flavours and textures make meals a delight to the eye and palate. Served up as side dishes or accompaniments to staples and main dishes, vegetables are a vital component of every healthy diet.

Nutrient Power
Vegetables contribute a host of vitamins, minerals, fibre and phytonutrients to the diet. They are also naturally low in calories and sodium. There is scientific evidence to show that diets rich in vegetables, fruit and whole grains provide protection against common lifestyle related diseases such as heart disease, type 2 diabetes and certain cancers.

Healthier Choices
Encourage your children to eat vegetables, and a wide variety of them, especially the colourful ones. Every natural hue — green, yellow, orange, red, purple and white — offers unique health benefits. Refer to the table on the facing page for more detail.

Portion Ration
Aim for two servings of vegetables every day. A serving of vegetables is about a three-quarter cup of cooked vegetables. Build small portions into the regular meals and snacks that your tweens consume to achieve the recommended amount each day.

Choices of Vital Veggies
- Mushrooms
- Ladies fingers (okra)
- Broccoli
- Cauliflower
- Carrots
- Bittergourd
- Potatoes
- Sweetcorn
- Celery
- Spinach
- Green peas
- Cabbages
- Asparagus
- Sweet potatoes
- Pumpkin
- Beans
- Yam
- Tomatoes

Colour	Phytonutrients	Potential Benefits	Vegetables
Blue and purple	Anthocyanins Polyphenols	• Lowers risk of some cancers* • Maintains urinary tract health • Supports memory functions	Purple cabbages, aubergines (eggplants), potatoes (purple-fleshed variety)
Green	Lutein Indoles	• Maintains vision health • Supports bone and teeth strength • Lowers risk of some cancers*	Broccoli, cabbages, green beans, celery, leafy greens (e.g. spinach and lettuce), ladies fingers (okra), peas, green capsicums (bell peppers)
Blue	Allicin	• Supports heart health • Maintains cholesterol levels that are already healthy • Lowers risk of some cancers*	Cauliflower, garlic, turnip (jicama), white mushrooms, onions, potatoes (white-fleshed variety)
Yellow and orange	Carotenoids Bioflavonoids	• Supports heart health • Maintains vision health • Supports healthy immune functioning • Lowers risk of some cancers*	Carrots, yellow capsicums (bell peppers), yellow potatoes, pumpkins, sweetcorn
Red	Lycopene Anthocyanins	• Supports heart health • Supports memory function • Lowers risk of some cancers* • Maintains urinary tract health	Red capsicums (bell peppers), red potatoes, tomatoes

* Low-fat diets rich in fruit and vegetables and low in saturated fat and cholesterol may reduce the risk of some types of cancer, a disease associated with many factors.

Source: USDA, 5 A Day Program

Dazzling Dairy

Milk, yoghurt and cheese are a rich source of many nutrients. While some children may have milk allergies or are lactose intolerant, most can include these products regularly in their diet.

Nutrient Power
The best-known nutrient in milk is calcium. Children need sufficient calcium to build strong bones and teeth. Milk is also a great source of good quality protein to support growth and repair. It also contains vitamin A and many B vitamins, and minerals such as phosphorus, magnesium and zinc. Many milk products are fortified with vitamin D, which helps enhance the absorption of calcium.

Healthier Choices
A wide variety of milk products are available for your children to include in their diet. Some are lower in fat, while others have added nutrients. So which is the best one for your children? Your choice should be guided by your children's regular diet. If they consume many high fat foods throughout the day, select a lower fat milk product. If your family enjoys a low-fat diet most of the time, then your children may need a full fat milk to support growth.

Portion Ration
Include at least one serving of dairy foods in your children's diet every day. A serving of dairy food is described as two glasses (500 ml / 16 fl oz) of milk, two slices of cheese (50 g / 1²/₃ oz) or two cups of yoghurt (500 ml / 16 fl oz).

Choices of Dazzling Dairy
- Skimmed and low-fat milk
- Skimmed and low-fat yoghurt
- Low-fat cheese

Magnificent Meats

Enjoyed for their texture and flavour, meats are a popular addition to main meals and some snacks.

Nutrient Power
Animal foods provide protein and many minerals such as iron, zinc and phosphorus. They are great sources of vitamin A and many B vitamins.

Healthier Choices
Lean and low fat choices are the best. These healthier options deliver the vital nutrients with less calories, fat, saturated fat, trans fat and cholesterol.

Portion Ration
A well-balanced diet can include up to two servings from this food group. A serving of cooked meat, fish or chicken is visually defined as the size of an average woman's palm or about 90 g (3¹/₆ oz). Include one to two servings of fish that are rich in Omega-3 fats such as salmon, tuna and mackerel in your family's diet every day. With seafood items, such as cooked prawns, cuttlefish and crabs, the portion recommended is also about 90 g (3¹/₆ oz).

Choices of Magnificent Meats
- Lean beef
- Chicken without skin
- Lean lamb
- Lean pork
- Fish, especially deep sea fishes
- Seafood (e.g. prawns)
- Eggs

Brilliant Beans

Legumes are also known as lentils or dried beans. Whole and split varieties are popularly used in some cuisines. Nearer home, this would include Indian dhals and Chinese or Peranakan snacks and desserts.

Nutrient Power
Rich in protein, legumes, in contrast to animal foods, are very low in fat and saturated fat, and naturally free of cholesterol. They are a good source of many B vitamins, especially folic acid and minerals such as potassium, iron and magnesium. They are also rich in fibre and many phytonutrients.

Healthier Choices
Many beans are available canned. Buy those canned in water or brine rather than in oil or sauce.

Portion Ration
Vegetarians should aim for two servings of legumes every day to create a well-balanced diet. For those who include animal foods in their diet, replace one serving of meat (out of the two recommended) every day with plant proteins. A three-quarter cup of cooked lentils makes a serving of protein-rich food.

Choices of Brilliant Beans
- Garbanzo beans
- Kidney beans
- Lentils
- Soy beans
- Tempeh
- Tofu

Amazing Nuts and Seeds

Although known to be high in fat and calories, nuts and seeds, if used in moderation, add flavour, texture and many valuable nutrients to the dishes they are cooked in.

Nutrient Power

While they are rich in protein, most nuts and seeds are short of one amino acid, called lysine. Eaten as part of a diet that includes legumes and/or animal proteins, this shortfall is compensated. The fat in nuts and seeds is mostly unsaturated and so are considered heart-friendly.

Healthier Choices

Select nuts and seeds that are fresh and wholesome, and avoid eating rancid nuts and seeds. Choose products that are prepared with less salt and sugar. Lightly toasted nuts and seeds also make better choices.

Choices of Amazing Nuts and Seeds

- Almonds
- Cashew nuts
- Sunflower seeds
- Peanuts

Fabulous Fruit

Fruit can be enjoyed as part of a main meal, snack or beverage. Fresh whole fruit is the most nutritious choice, but dried fruit, such as raisins, dates, figs and apricots, can be eaten as snacks or added to recipes to enhance the flavour and natural sweetness of the final dish.

Nutrient Power
Naturally full of many vitamins, minerals, fibre and phytonutrients, fresh fruit should be made a part of the diet of healthy children.

Healthier Choices
Like colourful vegetables, the colours of fruit — green, yellow, orange, red, purple and white — offer unique wellness values. Refer to the table below for more detail.

Portion Ration
Encourage your tweens to consume two servings of fruit each day. A serving of fruit is defined as one small apple, orange, pear or mango, one wedge (130 g / 4^1/$_2$ oz) of papaya, pineapple or watermelon, 10 grapes or longans, one medium banana, a quarter cup (40 g / 1^1/$_2$ oz) of dried fruit or one cup (250 ml / 8 fl oz) of pure fruit juice.

Colour	Fruit
Blue and purple	Purple grapes, blueberries, blackcurrants
Green	Green apples (with skin), green grapes, honeydew, kiwi fruit, green pears (with skin), guava (with skin), green mangoes
Blue	Bananas, pears, longans, lychees, mangosteens, rambutans
Yellow and orange	Oranges, papayas, mangoes, rockmelons, golden kiwi fruit, persimmons
Red	Watermelons, pomegranates, strawberries, red apples

Sample Meal Planner

Good meal planning will help you serve up nutritious and delicious meals and snacks that are attractive and interesting, especially for tweens. Here are some tips to bear in mind when planning a menu.

Plan your family's meals to serve up nutritious yet tasty and attractive dishes that will make meal times a happy affair!

1. Aim for Variety
Variety is the spice of life, so be brave and adventurous. Introduce your tween to many different wholesome foods and healthy cooking styles.

2. Achieve Nutritional Balance
Prepare food from the four food groups. Offer your children more wholegrains, vegetables and fruit, with moderate amounts of protein-rich foods such as meat, fish, chicken and milk. Keep added fat, sugar and salt low.

3. Make it Colourful
Colour attracts the eye and makes the meal interesting. Colourful fruit and vegetables are also nutrient-dense, so select naturally colourful foods to make your menu selection brilliant, both nutritionally and visually.

4. Ensure Contrast in Textures
Chewing contrasting food textures is enjoyable, so mix and match recipes to allow your children to enjoy many consistencies.

5. Serve Up Realistic Portions
Tweens have smaller tummies than adults do, so serve up small portions of wholesome foods to make up meals. Include nourishing snacks in between to add more nutrients to the diet.

day 1

Breakfast
Baked Banana
Delight
(page 47)
+
low-fat milk

Lunch
Tofu Burger
(page 89)
+
Kiwi and
Cucumber
Cooler
(page 35)

Snack
Fruity Macaroni
Energiser
(page 152)

Dinner
ABC Soup
(page 72)
+
Potato and
Spinach Patties
(page 119)
+
Seafood on
Skewers
(page 139)
+
rice

day 2

Breakfast
Tuna and
Veggie Wrap
(page 62)
+
calcium-fortified
soy milk

Lunch
Egg Noodles
with Sauce
(page 103)
+
Grape and
Coconut Delight
(page 39)

Snack
Fruit Kebabs
(page 150)

Dinner
Mushroom
Medley
(page 115)
+
Herb-crusted
Cod Fish
(page 132)
+
Chicken and
Corn Soup
(page 78)
+
rice

day 3

Breakfast
Fluffy Breakfast
Omelette
(page 85)
+
Papaya and
Carrot Smoothie
(page 35)

Lunch
Pizza Combo
(page 86)
+
Sunshine
Lollies
(page 159)

Snack
Choco Soy
Pudding
(page 149)

Dinner
Hearty
Pumpkin Soup
(page 71)
+
Seafood
Spaghetti
(page 90)

day 4

Breakfast
Savoury Oat
Porridge
(page 94)
+
Watermelon
Cooler
(page 40)

Lunch
Quick and Easy
Noodles
(page 101)

Snack
Easy Popcorn
(page 58)
+
Coco Nana
Shake
(page 36)

Dinner
Coriander
Chicken
(page 140)
+
Flower Power
(page 108)
+
Barley and
Yellow Cucumber
Pork Rib Soup
(page 80)
+
rice

day 5

Breakfast
Starry Pancake
Sandwiches
(page 44)
+
low-fat milk

Lunch
Cheesy
Macaroni with
Capsicum
(page 92)
+
Green Apple
and Coconut
Delight
(page 40)

Snack
Grilled Tuna
and Potato
Sandwich
(page 59)
+
Mango Sago
Surprise
(page 153)

Dinner
Mushroom Soup
(page 71)
+
Peas and Rice
(page 96)
+
Pork and
Veggie Roll
(page 143)

day 6

Breakfast
Raisin Muffins
(page 50)
+
low-fat milk

Lunch
Soupy Spinach
Noodles
(page 102)

Snack
Mini Cheese
and Ham Toasts
(page 55)
+
calcium-fortified
soy milk

Dinner
Fish and Tofu
Soup
(page 75)
+
Savoury
Meat Kebabs
(page 61)
+
French Bean
Surprise
(page 114)
+
rice

day 7

Breakfast
Peanut and Lean
Meat Porridge
(page 93)

Lunch
Claypot
Brown Rice
(page 98)
+
fresh fruit

Snack
Tasty Bites
(page 65)
+
Yummy
Yam Dream
(page 160)

Dinner
Veggie Rolls
(page 116)
+
Mild
Chicken Curry
(page 144)
+
Lemon
Cheesecake
(page 156)
+
rice

A well balanced diet of
regular meals and snacks
will keep tweens well
nourished to help them
perform at their best.

31

refreshing Beverages

Most kids love beverages, and plain water is the best beverage. Water hydrates and cools the body efficiently. Naturally calorie-free and easily available, it is the ultimate fluid for all. So, remember to offer your children water with meals and in between meals. It is also a good idea to encourage them to carry a water bottle everywhere they go!

Besides water, your children may want to drink many other delicious beverages. Educate and guide them to make the most nourishing choice. Beverages such as milk, fruit and vegetable juices, and milk shakes naturally contain lots of water and provide many valuable nutrients to the diet.

Juicing and blending are easy and practical ways to help your children enjoy fruit, vegetables, milk and yoghurt. On the flip side, whole fruit and vegetables have more fibre, vitamins and minerals than juices.

Juices are also not as satiating as whole fruit and kids may want to drink lots of it! Even if your children enjoy juices, keep the portion to no more than one serving each day. One serving is equivalent to 1 cup (250 ml / 8 fl oz).

Ideally, a nourishing beverage should have little or no added sugar. But there is no need to become didactic about sugar. A little, as part of a healthy and well-balanced diet, is okay. So, taste the beverages you prepare before giving them to your children. If they are very sour or very bland, add a little sugar to bring out the best of the natural flavours.

An electric juice extractor is a useful kitchen appliance for making juices. If you don't already own one and are thinking of getting one, select an electric juice extractor that retains some of the pulp or fibre. This way, your children will not miss out on the valuable nutrients found in fruit and vegetables.

Good Source: Vitamin K, Folate, Potassium
Excellent Source: Vitamin C, Vitamin A

Nutritional Analysis (per serving)

Energy 115 kcal   Saturated fat 0.5 g
Protein 4 g   Cholesterol 2.5 mg
Carbohydrate 25 g   Calcium 138 mg
Total fat 1.1 g   Iron 0.5 mg

Good Source: Manganese
Excellent Source: Vitamin C

Nutritional Analysis (per serving)

Energy 182 kcal   Saturated fat 0 g
Protein 2 g   Cholesterol 0 mg
Carbohydrate 40 g   Calcium 68 mg
Total fat 1 g   Iron 1.2 mg

papaya and carrot smoothie

This orange-coloured drink is a delight to both the eye and palate.

Carrots 3 (400 g / 14$^1/_3$ oz), washed
Papaya $^1/_2$ medium (500 g / 1 lb 1$^1/_2$ oz), skin removed
Low-fat yoghurt $^2/_3$ cup (160 ml / 5 fl oz)
Sugar (optional) 2 Tbsp

Cut carrots and papaya into pieces. Place in a juice extractor to extract juice, then pour into a blender with yoghurt. Blend, then taste and add sugar if necessary.

Pour into 4 glasses over ice cubes, if desired, and serve immediately.

kiwi and cucumber cooler

Once tweens take a sip of this pale green, naturally sweet and tangy beverage, they will love it!

Cucumber 1 medium (440 g / 15$^1/_2$ oz), chilled
Green kiwi fruit 4 (500 g / 1 lb 1$^1/_2$ oz), chilled
Pineapple 1 (600 g / 1 lb 5$^1/_3$ oz), chilled

Peel kiwi fruit and pineapple, then cut into pieces. Cut cucumber, into pieces.

Place cut ingredients into a juice extractor to extract juice. Pour into 4 glasses over ice cubes, if desired, and serve immediately.

4 pax

10 min

nutrition fact
Papayas and carrots are excellent sources of vitamin A and fibre. Vitamin A is essential for the maintenance of healthy vision, good skin and the immune system.

4 pax

10 min

nutrition fact
Kiwi fruit and cucumbers are great sources of fluid, which is essential for active children. Kiwi fruit has a high vitamin C content.

cooking tip
Keep the skin on the cucumber while juicing. It will help to enhance the colour of the beverage.

4 pax

5 min

cocoa nana shake

Combining the goodness of milk, yoghurt and bananas, this rich cocoa drink is a nourishing pick-me-up. It is a filling beverage on its own, but can be served with a hearty snack.

Low-fat evaporated milk 1 cup (250 ml / 8 fl oz), chilled
Low-fat yoghurt 1 cup (250 ml / 8 fl oz), chilled
Banana 1 medium (100 g / 3^1/$_2$ oz), peeled
Cocoa powder 2 Tbsp
Brown sugar (optional) 2 Tbsp

Garnish
Cocoa powder
Dark chocolate shavings

Place evaporated milk, yoghurt, banana, cocoa powder and brown sugar into a blender and process until smooth and well aerated.

Pour out into 4 cups over ice cubes, if desired. Garnish with cocoa powder and dark chocolate shavings. Serve immediately.

Good Source: Phosphorus
Excellent Source: Calcium

Nutritional Analysis (per serving)

Energy 134 kcal	Saturated fat 0.8 g
Protein 9 g	Cholesterol 4 mg
Carbohydrate 23 g	Calcium 303 mg
Total fat 1.5 g	Iron 0.8 mg

Source: Manganese

Nutritional Analysis (per serving)

Energy 131 kcal	Saturated fat 0 g
Protein 1 g	Cholesterol 0 mg
Carbohydrate 32 g	Calcium 36 mg
Total fat 0.5 g	Iron 0.9 mg

Grape and coconut delight

This rich amethyst coloured drink, livened up with 'iced-grapes' will be quite a talking point for the kids.

Seedless red grapes 700 g (1$\frac{1}{2}$ lb) + more for freezing
Tender coconut water 2 cups (500 ml / 16 fl oz)
Tender coconut flesh 100 g (3$\frac{1}{2}$ oz), cut into strips

Place some grapes in the freezer and leave overnight until frozen.

Place grapes in a juice extractor and extract about 2 cups (500 ml / 16 fl oz) juice. Use more grapes if necessary. Mix with tender coconut water.

Pour into 4 glasses over frozen grapes and ice cubes, if desired. Add tender coconut flesh and serve immediately.

nutrition fact

Purple grapes are celebrated for their natural resveratrol content. Resveratrol is a potent antioxidant that may support heart health and prevent some types of cancer. Grapes also have many other phytonutrients and are a source of vitamin C.

4 pax

12 min

nutrition fact
Does watermelon raise blood sugar sky high? Watermelons have a high Glycemic Index (GI) but the Glycemic Load (GL) is low. This means that in the portion normally eaten, watermelon does not raise blood sugar any more than many other fruit!

Watermelon packs a powerful lycopene punch. Lycopene is the pigment that colours fruit like watermelons and tomatoes. It is an antioxidant that neutralises active free radical molecules that may damage cells and cell walls, if left unchecked. Watermelons contain 40% more lycopenes than tomatoes!

4 pax

12 min

nutrition fact
Tender coconut water is a great fluid for active kids as it is a natural source of many electrolytes, the substance that helps maintain the body's fluid balance. Coconut water is also a source of calcium, magnesium, phosphorus and potassium.

cooking tip
Add a teaspoon of lime juice to prevent green apple juice from turning brown.

watermelon cooler

Use ripe red watermelons when making this beverage. They are simply sweeter and more nutritious than fruit that are paler in colour.

Celery 4 stalks (200 g / 7 oz), chilled
Watermelon 600 g (1 lb 5$^1/_3$ oz), chilled
Fresh lemon juice 6 tsp
Sugar (optional) to taste

Cut celery into pieces. Scoop out watermelon flesh. Place celery and watermelon into a juice extractor to extract juice.

Mix juices and taste. Add sugar if necessary and stir well. Pour into 4 glasses over ice cubes, if desired. Garnish with lemon slices if desired. Serve immediately.

Green apple and coconut delight

Mature coconut flesh is high in fat, but tender coconut flesh is not.

Green apples 6
Tender coconut water 2 cups (500 ml / 16 fl oz)
Ice cubes (optional)
Tender coconut flesh 100 g (3$^1/_2$ oz), cut into strips

Place apples in a juice extractor and extract about 2 cups (500 ml / 16 fl oz) juice. Mix with coconut water.

Pour into 4 glasses over ice cubes, if desired. Add coconut flesh and serve immediately.

Source: Vitamin A, Vitamin K
Good Source: Vitamin C

Nutritional Analysis (per serving)

Energy 54 kcal   Saturated fat 0 g
Protein 1 g   Cholesterol 0 mg
Carbohydrate 13 g   Calcium 31 mg
Total fat 0.3 g   Iron 0.5 mg

Nutritional Analysis (per serving)

Energy 95 kcal   Saturated fat 0 g
Protein 0 g   Cholesterol 0 mg
Carbohydrate 23 g   Calcium 31 mg
Total fat 0.5 g   Iron 0.9 mg

super snacks

Tweens have smaller stomachs than adults do. As such, they cannot eat a lot at any one time!

Children grow rapidly, and their need for energy and nutrients is high. Three main meals may not be sufficient to supply them with all they need, so offer them snacks throughout the day.

Healthy snacks are like mini meals. To nourish your children well, offer a wide variety of healthy snacks. Think up creative ways in which you can deliver whole grains, fruit, vegetables and dairy products to make the snack count for more value. Limit fat and added sugar to keep the calorie intake low. Sodium-containing seasonings like salt and sauces should also be used in small portions to train your children to enjoy the natural taste of food.

Keep the serving size of snack portions small, about one-third to one-half of a portion you may serve up at breakfast. Overeating may spoil your children's appetite for main meals. Try to time snacks well. Offer these nourishing bites midway between main meals, so your children will still be able to work up enough appetite for lunch or dinner.

starry pancake sandwiches

In terms of nutritional value, these pancakes are a cut above those available off the shelf or in fast food restaurants. Low in fat and rich in fibre, serve them as a snack or a light breakfast accompaniment.

Fine wholemeal flour (atta) 150 g ($5^1/_3$ oz), sifted

Salt a pinch

Brown sugar $1^1/_2$ Tbsp

Double action baking powder $^1/_2$ tsp

Water $1^1/_2$ cups (375 ml / 12 fl oz)

Cooking oil as needed

Filling

Low-fat peanut butter 4 Tbsp

Strawberry jam
  (without added sugar) 4 Tbsp

Mix flour with salt, sugar, baking powder and water to form a thin batter. Leave batter to rest for 15 minutes.

Coat a non-stick pan lightly with oil. Pour 2 Tbsp batter into a star-shaped mould. Alternatively, omit mould and simply pour batter into pan for round pancakes.

Allow pancake to cook on one side before flipping it over to cook on the other side. Remove when done and keep warm. Repeat until ingredients are used up. Makes about 16 small pancakes.

Spread a pancake with peanut butter and top with strawberry jam. Cover with another pancake. Repeat to make 8 sandwiches. Serve warm.

note: Atta is a very fine-grain wholemeal flour typically used to make chapatti. It is available at Indian grocery stores.

Source: Niacin, Phosphorus, Magnesium
Good Source: Selenium
Excellent Source: Manganese

Nutritional Analysis (per serving)

Energy 295 kcal	Saturated fat 1.6 g
Protein 10 g	Cholesterol 47 mg
Carbohydrate 51 g	Calcium 49 mg
Dietary fibre 5.6 g	Iron 2.2 mg
Total fat 6.9 g	

Source: Magnesium
Good Source: Vitamin B₆, Vitamin A
Excellent Source: Vitamin C

Nutritional Analysis (per serving)

Energy 260 kcal	Saturated fat 0.5 g
Protein 3 g	Cholesterol 0 mg
Carbohydrate 65 g	Calcium 7 mg
Dietary fibre 4.6 g	Iron 1.2 mg
Total fat 1.9 g	

Baked Banana delight

Plantains look like large bananas. They are available in Asian markets all year round. Baking plantain softens the fruit and releases a natural sweetness. This combination of soft, sweet plantain topped with crunchy, caramelised coconut is truly irresistible.

Olive oil 1 tsp
Large plantains 2 (800 g / 1³/₄ lb) peeled and sliced
Lemon juice 2 tsp
Grated skinned coconut 2 Tbsp
Brown sugar 1 tsp

Preheat oven to 180°C (350°F).

Brush 4 small ovenproof dishes with oil, then arrange plantain slices in a layer in dishes.

Drizzle lemon juice over plantain slices, then sprinkle with grated coconut and brown sugar.

Place ovenproof dishes on a baking tray and place in the oven for 20 minutes, or until plantains are cooked and soft, and topping is lightly browned in parts.

Remove from oven and place under a hot grill for 5 minutes to brown the top lightly, if desired. Leave to cool slightly, then serve warm. Be careful as dishes may still be hot.

4 pax

5 min

20–30 min

nutrition fact
Plantains are higher in potassium and vitamin A than regular bananas.

cooking tip
You can use regular bananas for this recipe as well. If so, choose firm bananas that are just ripening but not overripe.

4 pax

10 min

sweet puffed rice

This recipe is a sure shot way of getting children to eat a little more fruit. The bright colours of fresh fruit, cut into small cubes, topped with crunchy nuts, will attract most tweens. Involve your children in selecting the fruit assortment, chopping them up and then assembling the ingredients. You will have a more willing eater at the table.

Plain puffed rice $1^1/_3$ cup (20 g / $^2/_3$ oz)

Kiwi 1 (80 g / $2^4/_5$ oz), peeled and cut into cubes

Mango $^1/_2$ (100 g / $3^1/_2$ oz), peeled, stoned and cut into cubes

Persimmon $^1/_2$ (85 g / 3 oz), cut into cubes

Walnuts $^1/_4$ cup, toasted and chopped

Raw peanuts 1 Tbsp, toasted, skinned and chopped

Heat a non-stick pan and toast puffed rice for 3 minutes, stirring frequently.

To assemble, mix toasted puffed rice with fruit, then top with nuts. Serve immediately.

Good Source: Vitamin C

Nutritional Analysis (per serving)

Energy 87 kcal
Protein 2 g
Carbohydrate 16 g
Dietary fibre 2.3 g
Total fat 2.4 g

Saturated fat 0.3 g
Cholesterol 0 mg
Calcium 13 mg
Iron 1.9 mg

nutrition fact

Raisins are naturally low-fat, energy-dense snacks that can be eaten as is. Made by drying grapes, raisins are also loaded with antioxidants. Pack them into lunch boxes or add them to your recipes. Raisins are a great food but, like all good things must be taken in the right proportions. A serving size is made up of a quarter cup (40 g / 1 1/2 oz).

Nutritional Analysis
(per muffin)

Energy 97 kcal
Protein 2 g
Carbohydrate 16 g
Dietary fibre 0.4 g
Total fat 2.9 g
Saturated fat 1.7 g
Cholesterol 22 mg
Calcium 21 mg
Iron 0.3 mg

raisin muffins

Muffins are easy to eat on-the-go. These muffins get most of their sweetness from the raisins. Bake some ahead of time, then place two to four in well-sealed plastic bags and place in the freezer. Defrost and reheat as needed.

Self-raising flour 160 g (5 2/3 oz)
Salt 1/2 tsp
Castor (superfine) sugar 45 g (1 1/2 oz)
Double action baking powder 1 1/3 tsp
Raisins 2 Tbsp
Egg 1 (50 g / 1 2/3 oz)
Butter 2 1/2 Tbsp, melted and cooled
Non-fat milk 1/2 cup (125 ml / 4 fl oz)

Preheat oven to 200°C (400°F).

Sift flour, then add salt, sugar and baking powder and sift again into a mixing bowl. Add raisins and mix well.

In a separate bowl, beat egg, then add butter and milk. Add mixture to flour gradually and mix briefly for 10–20 seconds.

Portion batter equally into 12 paper muffin cups. Place in the oven and bake for 20 minutes, or until done. A skewer inserted into the middle of muffins should come out clean.

Remove from oven and serve warm.

never-fail chocolate cake

Most tweens love chocolate cake. This amazing recipe, leavened with yoghurt and bicarbonate of soda, makes a moist cake that is lower in fat and higher in calcium and protein, than cakes from supermarkets or bakeries. Follow the recipe carefully to get the best results.

Egg 1 (50 g / $1^2/_3$ oz)

Cocoa powder $1/_4$ cup (22 g / $^2/_3$ oz)

Butter 60 g (2 oz), softened

Plain (all-purpose) flour 1 cup (125 g / $4^1/_2$ oz)

Low-fat yoghurt $1/_4$ cup (60 ml / 2 fl oz)

Vanilla essence $1/_2$ tsp

Bicarbonate of soda $1/_3$ tsp

Sugar 220 g (8 oz)

Hot water $1/_4$ cup (60 ml / 2 fl oz)

Preheat oven to 180°C (350°F). Line a 20-cm (8-in) square cake tin with non-stick baking paper.

Measure out all ingredients exactly in the order listed above and add to a mixing bowl. Mix well into a smooth batter.

Pour batter into prepared cake tin and bake for 30–40 minutes, until a small skewer inserted into the centre of cake comes out clean.

Remove from oven and set aside to cool before removing from tin. Peel baking paper way, then cut into 12 slices to serve.

nutrition fact

Cocoa powder is used in this recipe as it is lower in fat and sugar content than prepared chocolate. It is also naturally rich in beneficial flavonoid antioxidants. Enjoy this cake in small portions, as a treat for special occasions.

Nutritional Analysis
(per slice)

Energy 154 kcal

Protein 2 g

Carbohydrate 27 g

Dietary fibre 0.9 g

Total fat 4.7 g

Saturated fat 2.7 g

Cholesterol 28 mg

Calcium 32 mg

Iron 0.8 mg

 20-cm (8-in) cake

 20 min

30–35 min

nutrition fact

Carrots are rich in soluble fibre and beta-carotene, the plant pigment that gives carrots their orange-yellow colour. Beta-carotene is transformed into vitamin A, as the body requires it. It also functions as a powerful antioxidant. The body absorbs beta-carotene much faster from carrots that are cooked rather than raw. This recipe omits butter and margarine to keep the saturated fat content lower, and replaces it with soy bean oil, a good source of unsaturated fats. Soy bean oil also contains Omega-3.

Excellent Source: Vitamin A

Nutritional Analysis
(per slice)

Energy 165 kcal
Protein 2 g
Carbohydrate 19 g
Dietary fibre 1 g
Total fat 9.8 g
Saturated fat 1.7 g
Cholesterol 23 mg
Calcium 38 mg
Iron 0.7 mg

carrot cake

This amazing cake recipe is chock-full of fibre and nutrients. It is one smart way of getting your tweens to eat carrots. Use atta when making this cake (see Note, page 44). Regular wholemeal flour from supermarkets has a coarser texture and will result in a very dense cake.

Fine wholemeal flour (atta) 95 g (3^1/$_3$ oz)

Baking powder 1 tsp

Salt ^{1}/$_2$ tsp

Ground cinnamon 1 tsp

Eggs 2 (100 g / 3^1/$_2$ oz)

Brown sugar 160 g (5^2/$_3$ oz)

Soy bean oil ^{1}/$_2$ cup (125 ml / 4 fl oz)

Carrots 1^1/$_2$ medium (250 g / 9 oz), peeled and finely grated

Raisins ^{1}/$_4$ cup

Walnuts ^{1}/$_2$ cup, chopped

Preheat oven to 200°C (400°F). Line a 20-cm (8-in) square cake tin with non-stick baking paper.

Sift flour, baking powder, salt and cinnamon into a mixing bowl.

Using an electric cake mixer, beat eggs, brown sugar and oil until well mixed. Fold in sifted ingredients, then add carrots, raisins and walnuts and fold in gently again.

Pour batter into cake tin and bake for 30–35 minutes, or until a small skewer inserted into the centre of cake comes out clean.

Remove from oven and set aside to cool before removing from tin. Peel off baking paper, then cut into 16 slices to serve.

cooking tip

Do not worry if it seems like there is too much carrot in the recipe when mixing the batter. This recipe ensures that you can taste and see the carrot even after baking.

chewy chocolate cookies

Kids adore cookies, but many popular recipes are high in sugar and fat, especially saturated fat and trans fat. Here is a simple cookie recipe that requires no added fat and is free of cholesterol. There is however still quite a bit of sugar, so offer your tweens just two at a time.

Icing (confectioner's) sugar 1 cup

Cocoa powder 1/2 cup

Plain (all-purpose) flour 1 Tbsp

Egg whites 2

Instant coffee powder 1/2 tsp (optional)

Water 1/2 Tbsp

Cashew nuts 1/2 cup, chopped

Preheat oven to 200°C (400°F). Line and grease some baking trays.

Sift sugar, flour and cocoa powder together.

Using a hand-held blender, whip egg whites until stiff, then fold in sugar and flour mixture until well mixed.

Mix coffee powder with water and stir into mixture. Fold in chopped cashew nuts.

Using a tablespoon, scoop up 1 Tbsp cookie dough and place a prepared baking tray. Repeat to make about 20 cookies in total. Place dough well apart as cookies will expand during baking.

Bake each batch of cookies for about 15 minutes until top of cookies are firm. The centres will remain soft. Remove from tray and leave to cool on a wire rack. Store in an airtight container.

cooking tip
Replace cashew nuts with walnuts or almonds for an interesting variation.

nutrition fact
Cashew nuts are a good source of many minerals especially magnesium, phosphorus, copper and manganese. Try to use only dry roasted or baked nuts and avoid those that are deep-fried, salted or covered with syrup.

Cocoa and coffee contain caffeine and each of these cookies provide about 5 mg caffeine. Many national health authorities recommend that for children aged 12 and under, the maximum daily caffeine intake should be no more than 2.5 mg per kilogramme of body weight. So, for children aged 7 to 9, keep the daily caffeine intake under 63 mg and for older children aged 10 to 12, keep it to less than 85 mg.

Nutritional Analysis
(per cookie)

Energy 48 kcal

Protein 1.3 g

Carbohydrate 7.2 g

Total fat 2.2 g

Saturated fat 0.4 g

Cholesterol 0 mg

Calcium 11 mg

Dietary fibre 0.9 g

Iron 0.5 mg

Source: Selenium
Good Source: Manganese

Nutritional Analysis (per serving)

Energy 148 kcal	Saturated fat 2.9 g
Protein 7 g	Cholesterol 49 mg
Carbohydrate 13 g	Calcium 79 mg
Dietary fibre 1.9 g	Iron 1.2 mg
Total fat 8.2 g	

mini cheese and ham toasts

Whip these up for a simple snack whenever there is a snack attack! These bite-size treats have a crispy base and a flavourful, moist golden brown topping.

Egg 1 (50 g / 1²/₃ oz)

Ground black pepper to taste

Grated Cheddar cheese 2 Tbsp

Lean honey baked ham 1 thin slice

Wholemeal bread 4 slices

Olive oil 1 Tbsp

Garnish

Yellow cherry tomatoes 4, sliced

Dill sprigs

Tomato sauce

Beat egg and season with pepper to taste. Add grated cheese and lean ham and stir lightly to mix.

Cut crust from bread, then cut each slice into 4 pieces. Heat a non-stick pan and coat with a little oil.

Dip one side of bread in egg mixture. Ensure that there is some cheese and ham on bread.

Place bread egg-side down onto heated pan. Cook 3–4 at a time depending on size of pan. Allow egg to cook on one side before turning bread over to brown other side.

Garnish with tomato slices and dill sprigs. Serve warm with tomato sauce on the side.

nutrition fact

Wholemeal bread is a healthier choice as it has more fibre, minerals, vitamins as well as antioxidants that are found in the germ and bran of a whole grain. Train your tweens to accept wholemeal bread early by making it the family's preferred choice. They will enjoy the natural nutty flavour and more substantial bite.

4 pax

15 min

salmon and seaweed rolls

The brilliant colours, fancy shapes and subtle flavours of Japanese foods are the in-thing for tweens. But, if you feel challenged by the numerous special ingredients you may need to make an authentic Japanese dish, start off with this simple spoof of a sushi roll. In this recipe, a slice of high fibre white bread replaces Japanese rice. It is easy and fast to prepare to satisfy a hungry tween!

Seaweed (nori) 2 sheets, cut lengthwise in half and toasted

High-fibre white bread 4 slices, crusts removed

Salmon 80 g (2⁴/₅ oz), thinly sliced

Cucumber 80 g (2⁴/₅ oz), cut into strips as long as bread

Light mayonnaise 2 tsp

Place a sheet of seaweed on a clean breadboard and lay a slice of bread over it. Layer with salmon and cucumber, then spread lightly with mayonnaise.

Roll up tightly from short side of seaweed. Fasten roll with toothpicks. Repeat to make more rolls until ingredients are used up.

Cut each roll into three. Arrange on a plate and serve immediately.

Good Source: Vitamin A

Nutritional Analysis (per serving)

Energy 110 kcal	Saturated fat 0.7 g
Protein 6 g	Cholesterol 13 mg
Carbohydrate 14 g	Calcium 36 mg
Dietary fibre 1.0 g	Iron 0.9 mg
Total fat 3.7 g	

4 pax

2 min

5–8 min

cooking tip

Popcorn can also be done in the microwave oven. Use a covered mircowave-safe dish or your oven will soon look like a battlefield! Place 1 Tbsp butter in the dish and cook on High for 30 seconds, then add 30 g (1 oz) corn kernels. Cover and cook for 3–5 minutes, stopping once or twice to give the bowl a shake. Vary the flavour of the popcorn. Sprinkle with cinnamon sugar or celery salt.

easy popcorn

Commercially available popcorn is coated with sugar and butter, or salt. But strip away the seasonings and you have a great ingredient — a whole corn kernel. Believe it or not, this is a whole grain! If your tweens still wrinkle their noses at wholemeal bread and brown rice, here is one 'whole' grain that they may accept without a whimper.

Olive oil 1^1/$_2$ Tbsp
Dried corn kernels ^{1}/$_4$ cup (50 g / 1^2/$_3$ oz)
Salt to taste

Use a large heavy-based frying pan with a ventilated lid.

Heat oil in pan and add corn kernels. Stir-fry until first kernel pops. Cover pan with lid, then shake pan over heat frequently until popping sound stops.

Sprinkle with salt and serve immediately.

Grilled tuna and potato sandwich

Sandwiches are quick and easy to put together. Start with wholemeal bread, then fill it up with healthful ingredients to make a complete and well-balanced snack or main meal. Just be creative! Here is an interesting blend to get you started.

Potato 1 small (75 g / $2^{1}/_{3}$ oz), scrubbed clean

Tuna canned in water 50 g ($1^{2}/_{3}$ oz), drained

Chives 1 tsp, finely chopped

Light mayonnaise 1 Tbsp

Wholemeal bread 4 slices

Bring a small pot of water to the boil and cook potato in its skin until soft. Drain and set aside to cool. Cut into small cubes.

Mix together potato cubes, tuna, chives and mayonnaise.

Place a slice of bread on a sandwich maker and top with half portion of the filling. Cover with another slice of bread and close toaster to make sandwich. When sandwich is sealed and surface is golden brown, remove from toaster. Repeat with remaining ingredients.

Alternatively, toast bread and make a regular sandwich with filling.

Slice in half to make 4 sandwiches. Serve warm.

nutrition fact

Tuna is a great source of protein and 'healthful' unsaturated fats, including a generous amount of Omega-3. The benefits of Omega-3 are manifold and it may even help to lower 'bad' cholesterol and raise 'good' cholesterol in the blood. Canned tuna is convenient and safe to eat. Make a healthier choice by selecting tuna canned in water or brine more often than products canned in oil or sauce.

Good Source: Selenium, Manganese

Nutritional Analysis (per serving)

Energy 102 kcal

Protein 6 g

Carbohydrate 15 g

Dietary fibre 2.2 g

Total fat 2.4 g

Saturated fat 0.5 g

Cholesterol 5 mg

Calcium 23 mg

Iron 1.2 mg

Source: Selenium
Good Source: Thiamin

Nutritional Analysis (per serving)

Energy 100 kcal   Saturated fat 1.3 g
Protein 11 g   Cholesterol 33 mg
Carbohydrate 2 g   Calcium 16 mg
Dietary fibre 0 g   Iron 0.6 mg
Total fat 5.2 g

savoury meat kebabs

A traditional Middle Eastern dish, kebabs are flavoured meats that are moulded on a skewer, then grilled or broiled. Pick a meat of your choice and make fresh kebabs to replace processed sausages at home. In this recipe, yoghurt is used as a tenderiser.

Lean minced meat (pork, beef or lamb) 200 g (7 oz)

Plain low-fat yoghurt 1 1/2 Tbsp

Garlic paste 1 tsp

Garam masala (Indian spice mix) 1/2 tsp

Lemon juice 1/2 tsp

Corn flour (cornstarch) 1/2 Tbsp

Coriander leaves (cilantro) 1 Tbsp, finely chopped

Salt and ground black pepper to taste

Olive oil 1 Tbsp

Preheat oven to 220°C (440°F).

Combine minced meat, yoghurt, garlic, garam masala, lemon juice, corn flour, coriander leaves in a bowl. Season with salt and pepper.

Divide mixture into 8 equal portions, then wrap each portion around a bamboo skewer.

Coat a flat pan with olive oil, then place kebabs in pan. Brown kebabs lightly on one side, then turn over to brown other side.

Transfer browned kebabs to an oven tray and bake for 10 minutes, or until meat is well cooked.

Remove kebabs from skewers, if desired and serve warm.

4 pax

10 min

20 min

nutrition fact

Lean meat is a great source of protein, many B vitamins and iron. Select a lean cut and ask the butcher to mince it. This way you can be sure it is not embedded with fat. The challenge to cooking with lean meat is that it has less flavour than fatty meat and tends to get tough when cooked. So, pep up the flavour with natural herbs and spices and tenderise lean meat with yoghurt or raw papaya or pineapple before cooking.

cooking tip

To save time when cooking, prepare basic ingredients such as garlic and ginger beforehand. Peel larger quantities of garlic or ginger and place in a blender to purée. Store refrigerated and use when needed.

4 pax

50 min

20 min

tuna and veggie wrap

Popiah and chapatti, both well-loved dishes in Chinese and Indian cuisines, are the inspirations that led to the creation of this recipe. Expose your tweens to the wide variety of Asian foods and eating cultures, and make it part of their regular lifestyle. They will be culturally richer for it!

Wrap

Fine wholemeal flour (atta) 100 g (3^1/$_2$ oz)

Salt a pinch

Corn oil 1 Tbsp

Water 80–100 ml (2^2/$_3$–3^1/$_3$ fl oz)

Filling

Corn oil 1 Tbsp

Garlic 1 clove, peeled and finely ground

Meat curry powder ^{1}/$_4$ tsp

Turnip 50 g (1^2/$_3$ oz)

Carrot 20 g (^{2}/$_3$ oz)

Cucumber 50 g (1^2/$_3$ oz)

Tuna canned in water 100 g (3^1/$_2$ oz), drained

Salt to taste

Coriander leaves (cilantro) 1 sprig, finely chopped

Lettuce 4 leaves

Prepare wrap. Combine flour, salt and oil. Add water gradually until a smooth, pliable dough is achieved. Cover and set aside for 30 minutes. Divide dough into 8 portions and roll out each portion into a flat disc, about 20-cm (8-in) wide. Heat a frying pan and cook chapattis on one side until brown spots appear before flipping it over to cook other side. Repeat until chapattis are done. Keep warm.

Heat oil in a heavy-based pan and stir-fry garlic and curry powder until fragrant. Add turnip. carrot, cucumber and tuna. Mix well and season with salt. Remove from heat. Garnish with coriander leaves, if desired.

To assemble, divide filling into 8 portions and drain well. Place a lettuce leaf on a chapatti, then top with a portion of filling. Fold chapatti over. Repeat until ingredients are used up. Serve immediately.

Source: Niacin, Vitamin A
Good Source: Manganese
Excellent Source: Selenium

Nutritional Analysis (per serving)

Energy 180 kcal	Saturated fat 1.5 g
Protein 10 g	Cholesterol 8 mg
Carbohydrate 20 g	Calcium 15 mg
Dietary fibre 3.8 g	Iron 1.4 mg
Total fat 7.5 g	

Nutritional Analysis (per serving)

Energy 166 kcal
Protein 8 g
Carbohydrate 26g
Dietary fibre 0.2 g
Total fat 3.2 g

Saturated fat 0.1 g
Cholesterol 4 mg
Calcium 17 mg
Iron 0.9 mg

tasty Bites

This amazing combination of smooth salmon spread on a crisp cream cracker, topped with juicy, fresh fruit presents a burst of delectable flavours on the tongue. Tweens will love it and so will adults! You may find yourself using this recipe when you have guests dropping by.

Non-fat cottage cheese 100 g (3$^1/_2$ oz)

Smoked salmon 1 slice (30 g / 1 oz)

Cream crackers 12

Pineapple 40 g (1$^1/_2$ oz), cut into small wedges

Seedless grapes 6, sliced in half

Parsley (optional)

Using a hand-held blender, blend cottage cheese with smoked salmon into a smooth paste.

Spoon paste into a piping bag and pipe some onto a cracker. Alternatively, just spread paste on crackers.

Garnish with pineapple, grape and parsley, if desired. Serve immediately.

nutrition fact

Tangy, sweet, juicy and refreshing are just a few adjectives that you may use to try to describe the wonderful taste of tropical pineapples. Pineapples are a good source of vitamins C, B$_1$ and B$_6$ and dietary fibre.

cooking tip

Bromelain, the natural pineapple enzyme, helps break down proteins and makes an effective and natural meat tenderiser.

nutrition fact

Sweet potatoes are rich in fibre and contain a fair bit of vitamins A and C, as well as minerals like potassium, magnesium and iron. They are also rich in many beneficial phytonutrients such as beta carotene, lutein and zeaxanthin.

Excellent Source:
Vitamin A

Nutritional Analysis
(per serving)

Energy 124 kcal
Protein 2 g
Carbohydrate 23 g
Dietary fibre 3.0 g
Total fat 3.4 g
Saturated fat 0.7 g
Cholesterol 0 mg
Calcium 32 mg
Iron 0.7 mg

cooking tip

To get the best nutritional value out of sweet potatoes, scrub them, then boil, steam, bake or grill with the skin on. Cooking makes the sweet potato flesh softer and sweeter. Dare your tweens to eat the skin! It is good for them.

sweet potato cubes

Often overlooked in the past, sweet potatoes are now celebrated as a healthy root vegetable. Available in many hues ranging from yellow to orange and even purple, sweet potatoes add an accent to grace your table. Tweens will love this as a snack. You can even serve it up as the staple to complement a Western meal of roast meat and salad.

Orange flesh sweet potato 1 (200 g / 7 oz)
Yellow flesh sweet potato 1 (200 g / 7 oz)
Olive oil 1 Tbsp
Brown sugar 1 Tbsp

Bring a large pot of water to the boil and cook sweet potatoes until almost done. Drain and set aside to cool. Peel and cut into cubes.

Preheat oven to 250°C (475°F).

In a heavy-based pan, add oil and sugar. Allow sugar to caramelise slightly, then add sweet potato cubes. Stir to glaze sweet potato cubes.

Transfer sweet potato cubes to baking tray lined with non-stick baking paper. Place in the oven and bake for 20 minutes until edges of sweet potato cubes are golden.

Remove from oven and transfer to a serving plate. Serve warm as a snack.

savoury puffed rice and vegetables

This take on a traditional Indian street food, presents kids with a variety of colourful vegetables enhanced with crispy puffed rice and crunchy nuts. Prepare the ingredients, then let your children have fun assembling their own healthy treat.

Frozen corn kernels 1/4 cup (40 g / 1 1/2 oz)

Plain puffed rice 1 1/3 cup (20 g / 1 2/3 oz)

Cucumber 1/4 (75 g / 2 1/3 oz), cut into cubes

Tomato 1/2 (55 g / 2 oz), soft centre removed, cut into cubes

Peanuts 2 Tbsp, finely chopped

Coriander leaves (cilantro) 2 Tbsp, chopped

Rinse corn kernels in warm water and drain well.

Heat a non-stick pan and toast puffed rice for 3 minutes, stirring frequently.

To assemble, mix toasted puffed rice with corn kernels, cucumber and tomato. Garnish with peanuts and coriander leaves. Serve immediately.

nutrition fact

Cucumbers are naturally low in calories and adds bulk and crunch to salads. For better nutritional value, leave the skin on — it brings with it a lot more colour and a little more fibre.

Nutritional Analysis (per serving)

Energy 60 kcal

Protein 2 g

Carbohydrate 9 g

Dietary fibre 0.9 g

Total fat 2.4 g

Saturated fat 0.4 g

Cholesterol 0 mg

Calcium 10 mg

Iron 2.0 mg

cooking tip

Puffed rice is available from grocery stores that sell Indian ingredients. You can also use packaged cereal such as rice crispies or cornflakes.

hearty SOUPS

Soups are the ultimate comfort food for many tweens. Hearty broths are a great opener to lunch and dinner, and a welcome filler to keep your children going from one main meal to the next.

The secret to a good soup starts with a great stock. Try our basic homemade stock recipes (pages 74 and 81) to create delicious stocks. Make up a large pot of stock and store frozen or refrigerated. Having stock on hand makes cooking so much faster and easier. It also makes a great base for soups and sauces. Skim off the fat from the soup stock before adding it to your favourite recipe. The flavour of the stock should be obtained by slowly simmering the ingredients and not from using more salt or stock enhancers.

Soups are a great way to include lots of fluid in the diet of tweens. They are also a wonderful vehicle to add vegetables and milk into the diet of a fussy child. To ensure that soups are not just a welcome comfort food, make it nourishing by keeping a careful watch on the fat and sodium content.

Serving a large bowl of soup before a meal may fill up your children's stomachs and prevent them from eating the rest of the main meal. So keep the serving portion of soup moderate, about one cup full to start a meal, or serve it up Asian-style, along with the meal, and encourage your children to sip the soup throughout the meal.

Source: Vitamin C
Excellent Source: Vitamin A

Nutritional Analysis (per serving)

Energy 84 kcal	Saturated fat 0.7 g
Protein 3 g	Cholesterol 0 mg
Carbohydrate 12 g	Calcium 43 mg
Dietary fibre 1.0 g	Iron 1.4 mg
Total fat 3.9 g	

hearty pumpkin soup

Thick, smooth and rich, this savoury broth is delicious and filling. A child who refuses to eat vegetables may be persuaded to drink it. Take the cue from this soup and purée other cooked vegetables to make a soup to get the vegetable nourishment going. Peas, broccoli and carrots make great soups.

Pumpkin 500 g (1 lb 1¹/₂ oz), peeled, seeds removed and cut into chunks

Olive oil 1 Tbsp

Onion 1 medium (100 g / 3¹/₂ oz), peeled and finely minced

Garlic 2 cloves, peeled and finely minced

Homemade chicken stock (page 81) 3 cups (750 ml / 24 fl oz)

Salt and ground white pepper to taste

Low-fat plain yoghurt (optional)

Parsley

Steam pumpkin chunks until soft, then and mash until very smooth.

In a heavy-based stockpot, heat oil and stir fry onion and garlic until fragrant. Add chicken stock and mashed pumpkin. Stir well. Bring to the boil.

Ladle into bowls and garnish with a small spoonful of yoghurt and parsley, if desired. Serve hot.

4 pax

5 min

10 min

nutrition fact
Pumpkins are a good way to boost your tween's intake of beta-carotene and fibre.

cooking tip
Cut a slice of wholemeal bread into cubes. Toast them to make crispy croutons and serve with the soup.

4 pax

10 min

20 min

ABC soup

With kids, vegetables in soup and stews go down with more enthusiasm than a plate full of vegetables, no matter how well they are cooked or displayed. This simple soup features a host of brightly coloured vegetables and is enhanced with alphabet pasta for some pure fun.

Homemade chicken stock (page 81) 4 cups (1 litre / 32 fl oz)

Alphabet pasta 1/3 cup (60 g / 2 oz)

Potato 1 medium (170 g / 6 oz), washed and cut into cubes

Carrot 1 large (110 g / 4 oz), washed and cut into cubes

Frozen corn kernels 1/2 cup (70 g / 2 1/2 oz)

Tomato 1 medium (110 g / 4 oz), cut into wedges

Salt and ground white pepper to taste

Bring stock to the boil in a pot and add pasta, potato and carrot cubes. Cook until potato and carrot are just tender.

Add corn and tomato. Boil for another 5–8 minutes, until tomato is soft. Season with salt and pepper.

Remove from heat. Ladle into bowls and serve warm.

Source: Vitamin C, Selenium
Excellent Source: Vitamin A

Nutritional Analysis (per serving)

Energy 123 kcal	Saturated fat 0 g
Protein 4.4 g	Cholesterol 0 mg
Carbohydrate 26 g	Calcium 31 mg
Dietary fibre 2.8 g	Iron 1 mg
Total fat 0.8 g	

16 cups
(4 litres / 128 fl oz)

15 min

30 min

cooking tip

If you are using fatty fish like salmon for the Western style stock, place the fish bones on a flat pan and grill for 20 minutes at 250°C (475°F) until bones are brown before making stock. This will prevent the stock from becoming cloudy.

8 cups
(2 litres / 64 fl oz)

15 min

30 min

cooking tip

Keep to the boiling time stated in the recipe. Overboiling will cause the stock to pick up an unpleasant fishy taste.

74

homemade fish stock

Here are two simple fish stocks that you can prepare ahead of time — one takes a Western approach and the other, an Asian style of stock preparation. .

Western Style

Fish bones 1 kg (2 lb 3 oz)

Cold water 24 cups (6 litres / 192 fl oz)

Celery 1 stalk, chopped

Leeks 2 medium, chopped

Onion 1 medium, peeled and chopped

Carrot 1, chopped

Bay leaf 1

Parsley 3 stalks

Black peppercorns 5

Place all ingredients in a stockpot and bring to the boil. Lower heat and simmer uncovered for 20–30 minutes.

Remove pot from heat and strain stock. Use as needed, or leave to cool before refrigerating for up to 3 days. To keep stock for a longer period, freeze in small portions. Thaw as needed.

Asian Style

Water 9 cups (2.25 litres / 72 fl oz)

Dried anchovies (*ikan bilis*) 250 g (9 oz), washed and drained

Bring water to the boil in a stockpot. Add anchovies and lower heat to simmer. Cover and simmer for 30 minutes.

Remove pot from heat and strain stock. Use as needed, or leave to cool before refrigerating for up to 3 days. To keep stock for a longer period, freeze in small portions. Thaw as needed.

fish and tofu soup

The light soup made with a fish stock base is enhanced by a tinge of ginger to take away any 'fishy' smell or flavour. Finely flaked fish and light silken tofu add valuable protein to the dish. This makes a great start to a Chinese main meal.

Fish fillet (dory, mackerel or snapper) 100 g (3^1/$_2$ oz)
Light soy sauce 1 tsp
Ginger 1-cm (^{1}/$_2$-in) knob, peeled and finely shredded
Homemade fish stock (page 74) 3 cups (750 ml / 24 fl oz)
Salt and ground black pepper to taste
Silken tofu 150 g (5^1/$_3$ oz), cut into small cubes
Spring onion (scallion) 1, finely chopped

Place fish on a steaming plate and season with light soy sauce and half the shredded ginger. Place in a steamer and steam for 8–10 minutes until done. Remove and leave to cool. Flake fish finely.

Bring stock to the boil in a heavy-based stockpot. Season with remaining ginger, salt and pepper.

Add flaked fish and tofu. Allow stock to return to the boil, then remove from heat.

Ladle into bowls and garnish with spring onion, if desired. Serve hot.

4 pax

5 min

25 min

nutrition fact

Ginger is a herb, well-loved in Asian cuisine for its aroma and pungency. Traditional Asian medicine promotes ginger as a remedy for gastro-intestinal discomforts. Recent research suggests that it may helpful in preventing motion sickness.

Source: Phosphorus
Good Source: Vitamin B$_{12}$

Nutritional Analysis
(per serving)
Energy 89 kcal
Protein 11 g
Carbohydrate 2 g
Dietary fibre 0.1 g
Total fat 4 g
Saturated fat 1.0 g
Cholesterol 21 mg
Calcium 21 mg
Iron 0.5 mg

Source: Copper, Pantothenic Acid,
Phosphorus
Excellent Source: Vitamin D,
Manganese

Nutritional Analysis (per serving)

Energy 121 kcal	Saturated fat 0.2 g
Protein 6 g	Cholesterol 1 mg
Carbohydrate 17 g	Calcium 91 mg
Dietary fibre 3.3 g	Iron 1.3 mg
Total fat 4.1 g	

mushroom soup

Full of natural meaty flavour subtly enhanced by the fragrance of fresh mushrooms, this rich and creamy soup achieves its goals with very little added fat. Mushroom soup is one that most kids enjoy. Here we enhance it with a dash of oats for more fibre.

Homemade chicken stock (page 81) 1^1/$_2$ cups (375 ml / 12 fl oz)

Fresh button mushrooms 200 g (7 oz)

Fresh shiitake mushrooms 100 g (3^1/$_2$ oz)

Fresh oyster mushrooms 80 g (2^4/$_5$ oz)

Butter 1 Tbsp

Oats 3 Tbsp

Low-fat milk 1 cup (250 ml / 8 fl oz)

Salt and ground black pepper to taste

Bring stock to the boil in a pot. Add mushrooms and butter. Cook for about 10 mintes, then remove a few mushrooms for garnish, if desired. Keep stock on the boil.

In a separate bowl, mix oats with milk until smooth. Add gradually to boiling stock, stirring all the time.

Using a hand-held blender, blend all ingredients in the pot until smooth. Stir well and ladle into serving bowls.

Serve soup immediately, garnished with mushrooms.

4 pax

5 min

15 min

nutrition fact

Mushrooms are low in calories, carbohydrates and fat.
They are fair sources of the vitamins, riboflavin, niacin and pantothenic acid and minerals, copper and selenium. They also contain both soluble and insoluble fibres.

chicken and corn soup

Another hot favourite with kids, this soup has a meaty undertone that is set off by the natural sweetness of the corn. This thick soup goes well with a Western meal of roast chicken or lamb.

Homemade chicken stock (page 81) 3 cups (750 ml / 24 fl oz)
Canned creamed corn 400 g (14$^1/_3$ oz)
Salt and ground white pepper to taste
Egg 1, lightly beaten

In a heavy-based pan, mix stock with creamed corn. Bring to the boil and season with salt and pepper.

Slowly pour beaten egg into boiling soup, stirring all the time.

Remove from heat. Ladle into bowls and garnished as desired. Serve hot.

Nutritional Analysis (per serving)

Energy 75 kcal	Saturated fat 0.4 g
Protein 4 g	Cholesterol 47 mg
Carbohydrate 13 g	Calcium 31 mg
Dietary fibre 2 g	Iron 0.7 mg
Total fat 1.8 g	

4 pax

10 min

3 hr

nutrition fact

Barley is a whole grain. It is a great source of carbohydrates and good quality protein. It is naturally rich in dietary fibre, especially soluble fibre called beta-glucan. This fibre helps maintain a healthy blood cholesterol level, which in turn offers some heart health benefits.

Source: Thiamin, Selenium, Vitamin C

Nutritional Analysis (per serving)

Energy 144 kcal
Protein 7 g
Carbohydrate 9 g
Dietary fibre 3.9 g
Total fat 9.1 g
Saturated fat 3.3 g
Cholesterol 30 mg
Calcium 35 mg
Iron 0.9 mg

cooking tip

Vary this recipe by replacing pork ribs with bones of any other meat.

Barley and yellow cucumber pork rib soup

Pork rib soup is a traditional favourite in Chinese cuisine. Some homes enhance this broth by adding barley. Barley makes the broth a tad thicker, and the grains add interest to the soup. Eating the grains of barley is the only way to harness the benefit of this wholesome grain, so savour it and encourage your tweens to do so too.

Yellow cucumber 375 g (13^1/$_4$ oz)

Pearl barley 30 g (1 oz)

Pork ribs 150 g (5^1/$_3$ oz)

Red dates 8

Chinese wolfberries 2 Tbsp

Water 3 cups (750 ml / 24 fl oz)

Salt and ground white pepper to taste

Rinse all ingredients and set aside. Remove skin from yellow cucmber, then cut into cubes.

Place all ingredients in a large heavy-based stockpot. Bring to the boil, then lower heat and simmer for 3 hours.

Remove pork bones. Serve soup hot, to accompany a main meal.

homemade chicken stock

A good stock lays the foundation of a hearty soup and a full-bodied sauce. Vary meats, vegetables and herbs to create your own stock, one that your family enjoys. A flavourful stock will help you reduce the amount of salt you may need to add zest to your cooking.

Chicken 1 large (1.5–1.8 kg / 3 lb 4$\frac{1}{2}$ oz–4 lb)

Cold water 24 cups (6 litres / 192 fl oz)

Garlic 10 cloves, peeled and roughly pounded

Celery 5 stalks (400 g / 14$\frac{1}{3}$ oz), chopped

Leeks 2 medium (180 g / 6$\frac{1}{2}$ oz), chopped

Onions 2 medium (220 g / 8 oz), peeled and chopped

Carrots 2 large (150 g / 5$\frac{1}{3}$ oz), chopped

Bay leaves 3

Parsley 1 bunch (20 g / $\frac{2}{3}$ oz)

Black peppercorns 5

Remove skin and fat from chicken. Cut chicken into medium-size pieces. Rinse with cold water, then place into a large stockpot. Cover with cold water and bring to boil. When water boils, lower heat to a simmer. Skim off any scum that floats to the surface.

Add remaining ingredients and simmer uncovered, over low heat for 2 hours.

Remove from heat, strain stock and transfer to a clean pot. Leave to cool. When stock is cool, cover and refrigerate for a few hours or overnight.

Remove stock from refrigerator and spoon off any fat that has solidified on the surface of stock. Portion stock into small containers that can be chilled or frozen for use as needed.

wholesome main meals

Breakfast, lunch and dinner are the three main meals that most people include as part of their regular diet. These meals provide the largest share of nutrients to nourish the individual.

For school-going tweens, juggling school and extra-curricular activities sometimes makes it hard for them to sit down and eat a meal. But skipping meals means a huge loss of nutrients for the day. It may also cause hunger that leads to indiscriminate snacking.

Tweens should take part in family meals. Sharing meals together gives family members an opportunity to communicate and enjoy a sense of belonging. And tweens need a lot of that! So, no matter what your personal pressures are, make the effort to keep the family eating together as much as possible. It will also help you gauge your children's eating habits and food preferences, while giving you the opportunity to model healthy eating behaviour.

Healthy and well-balanced main meals should include all the four food groups — grains, vegetables, fruit and protein-rich foods. Select wholesome ingredients and use healthy cooking methods to whip up simple and nourishing main meals. Use less fat and added salt and sodium-containing seasonings to keep the dishes healthful.

Once you start cooking, you can pick up some amazing skills that will help you whip up great dishes that look good and taste great. Preparing family meals also gives you greater control over your child's nutrition.

Involve your tweens in planning the menu, shopping, preparing and serving meals. This will not only provide opportunities for you to educate your children about healthy food and healthy eating, it will also promote family bonding. You will also be imparting life-skills to your children, since cooking and eating are basic survival skills.

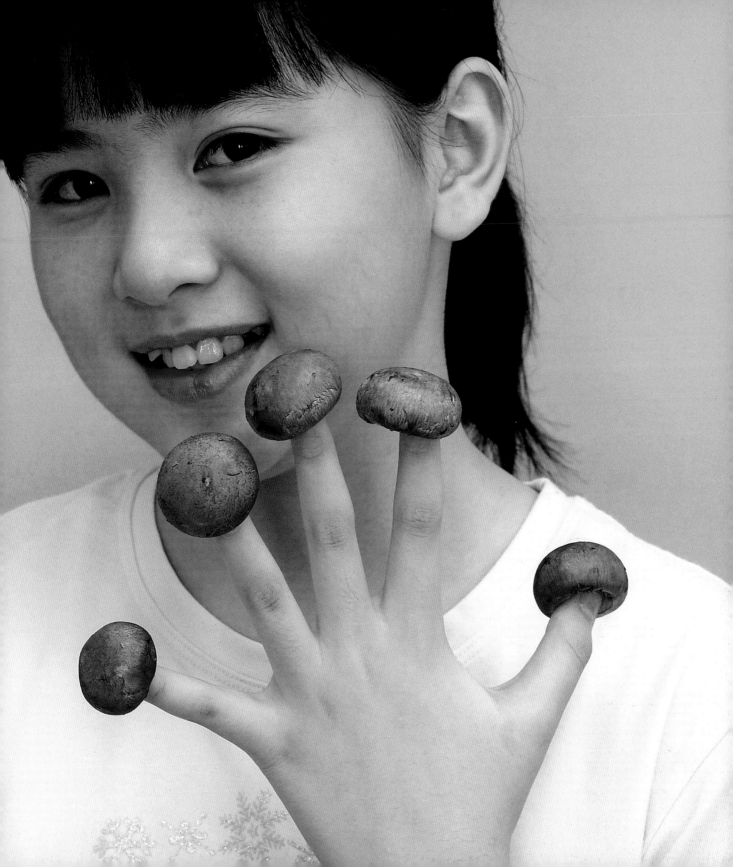

Source: Riboflavin, Phosphorus
Good Source: Selenium, Manganese

Nutritional Analysis (per serving)

Energy 165 kcal	Saturated fat 3.6 g
Protein 9 g	Cholesterol 194 mg
Carbohydrate 10 g	Carbohydrate 10 g
Dietary fibre 2.1 g	Calcium 100 mg
Total fat 10.3 g	Iron 1.8 mg

fluffy Breakfast omelette

Breakfast is an important meal. Start it off, occasionally, with this amazing omelette that is crispy on the outside and soft and mushy on the inside. Filled with vegetables and cheese, this fluffy breakfast omelette is simply scrumptious.

Eggs 4 medium (200 g / 7oz)

Salt and ground white pepper to taste

Olive oil 1 Tbsp

Tomato 1 large (165 g / 4^4/$_5$ oz), finely chopped

Green capsicum (bell pepper) ^{1}/$_4$ (30 g / 1oz), finely chopped

Button mushrooms 4, finely chopped

Grated Cheddar cheese 4 Tbsp

Accompaniments

Baked beans 8 Tbsp

Wholemeal bread 4 slices

Prepare one omelette at a time. Using one egg, separate egg white from yolk. Whip egg white until light and foamy, then add beaten egg yolk and whip until well mixed. Season with salt and pepper.

Heat a non-stick pan and coat lightly with oil. Add egg and swirl pan so egg covers base of pan. Cover with a tight-fitting lid and cook for 2 minutes.

Place one-quarter portion of chopped vegetables over omlette, then replace lid and cook for another 2 minutes.

Sprinkle 1 Tbsp grated cheese over omelette and cook until top of omelette is almost done. Fold omelette in half and remove to a serving plate. Repeat to make 3 more omelettes.

Serve hot, with baked beans and wholemeal bread.

nutrition fact

Eggs are an economical and excellent source of great quality protein. They are also a good source of selenium, iodine, phosphorus, vitamins B$_2$, B$_{12}$ and D, and choline, which is found in the membranes of cells, especially brain cells. Choline helps nerve cells communicate with each other.

cooking tip

To make the texture inside the omelette firmer, place it in a pre-heated oven set at 180°C (350°F) for 5 minutes.

4 pax

15 min

20–40 min

pizza combo

Pizza is popular with most tweens! Just select wholesome ingredients and transform their preferred food choice into a nourishing meal. Here is one way to do it.

Pizza bases 4 small, each about 100 g (3$\frac{1}{2}$ oz)
(use wholemeal, if available)

Tomato purée 8 Tbsp

Pineapple 116 g (4 oz), cut into cubes

Green capsicum (bell pepper) 1 small (120 g / 4$\frac{1}{4}$ oz),
cut into cubes

Button mushrooms 8, sliced

Lean ham 2 slices (50 g / 1$\frac{2}{3}$ oz), cut into strips

Prawns (shrimps) 100 g (3$\frac{1}{2}$ oz), each sliced in half

Crabsticks 2, sliced thinly

Low-fat grated mozzarella cheese 8 Tbsp

Preheat oven to 230°C (450°F).

Place pizza bases on a baking tray and spread with tomato purée. Top bases with pineapple, capsicum and mushrooms.

Top two pizza bases with ham and other two with prawns and crabsticks. Cover with mozzarella cheese.

Place baking tray in oven. Bake pizzas for 15 minutes until lightly browned and cheese is melted. Slice and serve hot.

Source: Vitamin A, Vitamin D, Zinc, Iron,
Thiamin, Niacin, Magnesium
Good Source: Calcium, Vitamin B6, Vitamin B12,
Copper, Phosphorus, Selenium
Excellent Source: Vitamin C, Manganese

Nutritional Analysis (per serving)

Energy 607 kcal   Saturated fat 4.2 g

Protein 36 g   Cholesterol 108 mg

Carbohydrate 32 g   Calcium 269 mg

Dietary fibre 4.7 g   Iron 3.6 mg

Total fat 10 g

Source: Vitamin K, Riboflavin, Magnesium, Phosphorus, Thiamin, Iron, Niacin
Good Source: Folate, Selenium, Vitamin A, Copper
Excellent Source: Calcium, Manganese

Nutritional Analysis (per serving)

Energy 358 kcal	Saturated fat 2.7 g
Protein 17 g	Calcium 507 mg
Carbohydrate 43 g	Cholesterol 0 mg
Dietary fibre 5.4 g	Iron 3.7 mg
Total fat 14.5 g	

tofu Burger

Kids love burgers! If you worry that they are eating too many of the high fat, high salt variety, slip this dish in on occasion to give them the wholesome goodness of soy and vegetables, presented in a wholemeal bun.

Firm tofu 1 square (140 g / 5 oz)

French beans 2, finely chopped

Carrot 1/3 medium, peeled and finely chopped

Dried Chinese mushrooms 4, soaked to soften, stems discarded, finely chopped

Coriander leaves (cilantro) 1 tsp, finely chopped

Spring onion (scallion) 1 tsp, finely chopped

Red and green chillies 1 tsp, finely chopped

Corn flour (cornstarch) 6 Tbsp

Salt and ground white pepper to taste

Rice bran oil 2 Tbsp

Mini wholemeal buns 8

Garnish

Lettuce leaves

Tomato 8 slices

Tomato ketchup (optional) 4 Tbsp

Mash tofu in a bowl. Add vegetables, herbs, corn flour, salt and pepper and mix well. Mould mixture into 8 patties.

Heat a pan and coat lightly with oil. Place patties in pan and cook until golden brown.

Cut wholemeal buns in half. Toast lightly if desired. Top bottom half of buns with a slice of tomato, some lettuce leaves, a tofu patty and more lettuce leaves, then cover with top half of bun.

Serve immediately with tomato ketchup on the side.

nutrition fact

Tofu is an amazing local food that is a great source of protein, calcium, manganese and iron. It also contains a fair bit of unsaturated fat, including Omega-3. The recent discovery of the unique heart health benefits of soy protein makes it a great choice to include in the diet of growing kids.

seafood spaghetti

Take tweens to a Western restaurant and you will find that spaghetti is a popular food choice. Why not plate up your own spaghetti at home for the whole family? It'll be tasty and fun!

Olive oil 2 Tbsp
Salt and ground white pepper
Angel hair pasta 150 g (5^1/$_3$ oz)
White fish (e.g. mackerel) 120 g (4^1/$_4$ oz), cut into cubes
Prawns (shrimps) 100 g (3^1/$_2$ oz), peeled and deveined
Squid 80 g (2^4/$_5$ oz), cleaned and cut into small pieces

Sauce
Olive oil 1 Tbsp
Onions 2, medium, peeled and finely minced
Garlic 6 cloves, peeled and finely minced
Carrot ^{1}/$_2$, medium, peeled and finely minced
Celery ^{1}/$_2$ stalk, finely minced
Red tomatoes 6 large, skinned and puréed
Mixed herbs ^{1}/$_2$ tsp, freshly chopped
Salt and ground white pepper to taste

Garnish
Low-fat mozzarella cheese 50 g (1^2/$_3$ oz), grated

Bring a large pot of water to the boil. Add 1 Tbsp olive oil and ^{1}/$_2$ tsp salt, then add pasta and cook for 8 minutes. Drain and cool. Set aside.

Combine remaining olive oil, ^{1}/$_4$ tsp salt and ^{1}/$_4$ tsp pepper in a bowl and add seafood. Mix well and refrigerate for 20 minutes to marinate.

Prepare sauce. Heat oil in a pan and stir-fry onions and garlic until fragrant. Add carrot and celery and cook for another minute. Add tomato purée and season with herbs, salt and pepper. Set sauce aside.

Using a clean pan with a little oil, pan-fry marinated seafood separately.

Divide pasta into serving dishes and top with sauce and seafood. Sprinkle with mozzarella cheese. Serve immediately.

Source: Calcium, Vitamin K, Riboflavin, Copper, Iron, Niacin, Magnesium
Good Source: Vitamin B$_6$, Vitamin B$_{12}$, Vitamin C, Phosphorus, Manganese
Excellent Source: Vitamin A, Selenium

Nutritional Analysis (per serving)

Energy 350 kcal	Saturated fat 2.2 g
Protein 21 g	Cholesterol 83 mg
Carbohydrate 43 g	Calcium 86 mg
Dietary fibre 4.6 g	Iron 3.1 mg
Total fat 10.2 g	

4 pax

10 min

20 min

nutrition fact
Cheese is a good source of protein and calcium. When using cheese in cooking, select a lower fat variety to make the dish a nutrient-dense choice.

cheesy macaroni with capsicum

The scrumptious cheese sauce holds all the ingredients in this dish together, making it an ultimate comfort food. Serve it up with a hug and your children will soon be recharged for the next round of action!

Water 8 cups (2 litres / 64 fl oz)
Macaroni 2 cups (200 g / 7 oz)
Corn flour (cornstarch) 4 Tbsp
Homemade chicken stock (page 81) 2 cups (500 ml / 16 fl oz)
Butter 2 Tbsp
Green capsicum (bell pepper) 200 g (7 oz), cut into cubes
Red capsicum (bell pepper) 200 g (7 oz), cut into cubes
Salt and ground black pepper to taste
Honey baked ham 4 thick slices (200 g / 7 oz), sliced

Bring water to the boil in a large pot. Add macaroni with a pinch of salt. Cook for 8–10 minutes, or until just done. Drain and set aside in a bowl.

Mix corn flour with 100 ml (3¹/₃ fl oz) chicken stock and set aside.

Gently warm butter in a non-stick pan. Add capsicums and stir-fry for 1 minute. Add remaining chicken stock and season with salt and pepper.

Stir in corn flour slurry and cook until sauce thickens. Pour sauce over cooked macaroni. Sprinkle ham over and serve warm.

peanut and lean meat porridge

Rice porridge with minced meat is an age-old Chinese favourite. Once considered a 'poor' man's food, porridge is a proud offering in many fine Chinese restaurants today. Replace pork with other meats of choice to make a dish that suits your tween's preference. Serve it as a light breakfast or lunch.

Lean minced pork 100 g (3^1/$_2$ oz)

Sesame oil ^{1}/$_2$ tsp

Light soy sauce ^{1}/$_2$ tsp

Brown rice 1 cup (200 g / 7 oz), washed and drained

Water 10 cups (2.5 litres / 80 fl oz)

Ginger (optional) 0.5-cm (^{1}/$_4$-in) knob, peeled and thinly sliced

Canned braised peanuts ^{1}/$_2$ can (55 g / 2 oz), drained

Ground white pepper to taste

Marinate pork with sesame oil and light soy sauce. Set aside.

Boil brown rice with water in a heavy-based pan until rice is tender.

Add ginger and marinated pork. Stir well until pork is cooked. Add braised peanuts and cook for another minute. Season with pepper.

Ladle into bowls and garnish as desired. Serve hot.

nutrition fact

Peanuts are known to be high in fat, but this is mostly monounsaturated fat. The nut is a good source of protein, and combined with meat in this recipe, the quality of the protein is improved. Peanuts also contain powerful antioxidants such as vitamin E and resveratrol, the antioxidant found in grapes.

Source: Vitamin B$_6$, Copper, Niacin, Phosphorus
Good Source: Magnesium, Thiamin
Excellent Source: Manganese

Nutritional Analysis (per serving)
Energy 298 kcal
Protein 13 g
Carbohydrate 40 g
Dietary fibre 2.9 g
Total fat 10.0 g
Saturated fat 1.8 g
Cholesterol 17 mg
Calcium 42 mg
Iron 1.9 mg

nutrition fact

Oats are a great source of long-lasting carbohydrates and fibre, especially the soluble kind, called beta-glucan that may help maintain healthy blood cholesterol levels. Oats is also a good source of manganese and selenium.

savoury oat porridge

Most people think of oats as food for the sick. Others are familiar only with the sweet version, cooked with milk and sugar. This recipe uses oats in a traditional Chinese rice and meat porridge and the result is just delightful.

Lean minced pork 100 g (3^1/$_2$ oz)

Light soy sauce 1 Tbsp

Ground white pepper to taste

Water chestnuts 2, peeled and finely chopped

Homemade chicken stock (page 81) 2 cups (500 ml / 16 fl oz)

Water 1 cup (250 ml / 8 fl oz)

Ginger (optional) 0.3-cm (^{1}/$_8$-in) knob, peeled and thinly sliced

Oats 1 cup (80 g / 2^4/$_5$ oz)

Dried Chinese mushrooms 4, soaked to soften, stems discarded, thinly sliced

Carrot ^{1}/$_2$ medium, peeled and thinly sliced

Salt and ground white pepper to taste

Sesame oil (optional) 1 tsp

Marinate minced pork with light soy sauce and pepper. Leave for 10 minutes. Add water chestnuts and mix well. Shape mixture into 16 small balls and set aside.

Heat chicken stock and water in a pot. Add ginger and oats and cook until almost done. Add meat balls and cook until done.

Toss in mushrooms and cook for another 2 minutes. Add carrot and cook until tender but still crunchy. Taste and season with salt, pepper and sesame oil, as needed.

Ladle into bowls and garnish as desired. Serve hot.

Source: Thiamin
Good Source: Selenium, Manganese,
Vitamin A

Nutritional Analysis (per serving)

Energy 168 kcal   Saturated fat 2.2 g
Protein 9 g   Cholesterol 18 mg
Carbohydrate 18 g   Calcium 25 mg
Dietary fibre 2.8 g   Iron 1.5 mg
Total fat 6.9 g

peas and rice

This one-dish meal looks pretty and tastes yummy! Dry and light, it packs well into lunch boxes so your tweens can have a hearty and nourishing meal in school.

Long-grain white rice $3/4$ cup (150 g / $5^1/3$ oz), washed and drained

Water $1^1/4$ cups (300 ml / 10 fl oz)

Rice bran oil 2 Tbsp

Garlic 2 cloves, peeled and chopped

Fish cake 1 roll (140 g / 5 oz), cut into cubes

Frozen peas 1 cup (160 g / $5^2/3$ oz)

Salt to taste

Egg 1 (50 g / $1^2/3$ oz), lightly beaten

Place rice and water in a rice cooker and cook until done. Leave to cool.

Heat oil in a wok and stir-fry garlic until fragrant. Add fish cake and rice and stir-fry for 3 minutes. Add peas and cook for another 2 minutes. Season with salt.

Create a space in the centre of rice and add egg. Allow egg to set, then scramble. Mix rice and egg well. Dish out and serve hot.

Source: Vitamin K
Good Source: Manganese

Nutritional Analysis (per serving)

Energy 264 kcal   Saturated fat 1.8 g
Protein 10 g   Cholesterol 47 mg
Carbohydrate 34 g   Calcium 65 mg
Dietary fibre 1.8 g   Iron 1.9 mg
Total fat 9.4 g

4 pax

10 min

15 min

nutrition fact

Brown rice has twice the fibre of white rice. Milling and polishing the grain to make white rice destroys more than half of the vitamins B₃, B₁ and B₆, manganese, phosphorus, iron and all the essential fats.

Source: Riboflavin
Good Source: Vitamin D, Vitamin B₆, Panthothenic Acid, Zinc, Copper, Thiamin, Niacin, Phosphorus, Magnesium, Selenium
Excellent Source: Vitamin A, Manganese

Nutritional Analysis
(per serving)
Energy 480 kcal
Protein 23 g
Carbohydrate 69 g
Dietary fibre 5.0 g
Total fat 13.2 g
Saturated fat 3.0 g
Cholesterol 59 mg
Calcium 52 mg
Iron 2.9 mg

claypot Brown rice

A great way to introduce brown rice to the family. This recipe infuses the whole grain with intense flavours, making it irresistible!

Chicken drumsticks 4 (300 g / 11 oz), skinned and deboned, cut into cubes

Brown rice 1¹/₂ cups (280 g / 10 oz), washed, drained

Homemade chicken stock (page 81) 3 cups (750 ml / 24 fl oz)

Dark soy sauce 2¹/₂ tsp

Salt and ground white pepper to taste

Corn oil 1 Tbsp

Chopped garlic 1 Tbsp

Dried Chinese mushrooms 12, soaked to soften, stems discarded and sliced

Frozen mixed vegetables 1 cup (140 g / 5 oz)

Lettuce 6 leaves, thinly sliced

Dried anchovies (*ikan bilis*) 2 Tbsp

Marinade
Light and dark soy sauce ¹/₂ Tbsp each

Oyster sauce 1 Tbsp

Sesame oil 1 tsp

Sugar ¹/₂ tsp

Ground white pepper ¹/₄ tsp

Combine ingredients for marinate in a bowl. Add chicken and leave for 30 minutes.

Put brown rice and stock into a rice cooker. Mix in dark soy sauce, salt and pepper. Stir well, then set rice cooker to cook.

Heat oil in a wok and stir-fry garlic until fragrant. Add chicken, mushrooms and mixed vegetables and stir-fry until three-quarters done. Remove and place into rice cooker on top of rice without mixing. Continue cooking until rice and ingredients are done.

Place dried anchovies in the microwave oven and cook on High for 3 minutes, turning them once in between. Mix ingredients, anchovies and lettuce into rice. Garnish as desired and serve hot.

sunny rice

4 pax

10 min

20 min

Tweens will welcome this flavoured rice dish. Cooking rice with tomato purée and stock infuses each grain with an irresistible aroma and flavour. Serve with mildly flavoured vegetable and protein-rich dishes.

Olive oil 2 Tbsp

Onion 1 medium, peeled

Ginger paste 1 tsp

Garlic paste 1 tsp

Green chilli (optional) 1, finely minced

Cinnamon stick 2.5-cm (1-in)

Bay leaf 1

Basmati rice 1 cup (200 g / 7oz), washed, drained

Tomatoes 3, (350 g / 12 oz), skinned and puréed

Tomato purée 2 Tbsp

Homemade chicken stock (page 81) 1 cup (250 ml / 8 fl oz)

Salt and ground white pepper to taste

Frozen mixed vegetables 1/2 cup (90 g / 3 1/6 oz)

Garnish

Lemon juice 2 Tbsp

Olive oil 1/2 Tbsp

Egg 1 (50 g / 1 2/3 oz), lightly beaten

Heat oil in a heavy-based wok and stir-fry onion, ginger, garlic and green chilli until fragrant. Add cinnamon and bay leaf and continue to fry for another minute. Add rice and stir well for another 2 minutes.

Transfer rice, puréed tomatoes, tomato purée and chicken stock into a rice cooker. Season to taste. Cook until rice is almost done, then add frozen vegetables and stir well. Continue to cook until rice and vegetables are just done.

Remove cinnamon stick and bay leaf. Sprinkle lemon juice and stir lightly.

Heat oil in a pan and add beaten egg. Swirl pan to form a thin omelette. Leave egg to set. Remove from pan and slice thinly.

Serve rice topped with sliced omelette.

nutrition fact

Basmati rice is enjoyed for its fragrance and subtle flavour. This long-grain rice does not raise blood sugar as much as other popular white rice grains.

Good Source: Vitamin A, Vitamin C, Manganese

Nutritional Analysis
(per serving)

Energy 286 kcal

Protein 6 g

Carbohydrate 49 g

Dietary fibre 2.8 g

Total fat 7.5 g

Saturated fat 1.5 g

Cholesterol 0 mg

Calcium 39 mg

Iron 1.1 mg

Source: Thiamin, Selenium, Manganese,
Phosphorus, Folate
Good Source: Vitamin A

Nutritional Analysis (per serving)

Energy 298 kcal	Saturated fat 1.8 g
Protein 8 g	Cholesterol 16 mg
Carbohydrate 46 g	Calcium 26 mg
Dietary fibre 2.0 g	Iron 1.1 mg
Total fat 8.6 g	

quick and easy noodles

Tweens adore noodles, and this recipe combines meat and vegetables, making it a complete meal. Serve as breakfast or a light lunch. It also packs well into lunch boxes.

Fine rice vermicelli (*beehoon*) 200 g (7 oz), soaked to soften, then drained

Lean pork 100 g (3^1/$_2$ oz), cut into thin strips

Canola oil 2 Tbsp

Onion ^{1}/$_2$ small, peeled and finely sliced

Garlic 2 cloves, peeld and finely minced

French beans 50 g (1^2/$_3$ oz), thinly sliced

Carrot 30 g (1 oz), cut into thin strips

Bean sprouts 100 g (3^1/$_2$ oz)

Salt and ground white pepper to taste

Marinade

Bottled vegetarian mushroom sauce 1 Tbsp

Sesame oil ^{1}/$_2$ tsp

Salt to taste

Bring some water to the boil in a large pot. Place rice vermicelli in to cook for 2–3 minutes. Drain vermicelli, then rinse with cold water and drain again. Set aside.

Combine ingredients for marinade in a bowl. Add pork and mix well.

Heat oil in a wok and stir-fry onion and garlic until fragrant. Add marinated pork and cook until done. Add French beans, carrot and bean sprouts and cook for 1–2 minutes until vegetables are tender but still crisp.

Add vermicelli and mix well. Season with salt and pepper and continue to stir-fry until done.

Dish out and serve hot.

nutrition fact

Fresh bean sprouts make a delicious and crunchy side dish, and it also goes well cooked with noodles. Germinated from mung beans or soy beans, bean sprouts are a good source of vitamin C.

4 pax

10 min

15 min

soupy spinach noodles

Noodle soup is a common dish prepared in many Asian homes. Accompany this dish with fruit or fruit juice to present your tweens with a well-balanced meal.

Dry spinach noodles 150 g (5$^{1}/_{3}$ oz)
Homemade chicken stock (page 81) 4 cups (1 litre / 32 fl oz)
Chicken 200 g (7 oz), skinned and deboned
Firm tofu $^{1}/_{2}$ square (100 g / 3$^{1}/_{2}$ oz)
Chye sim 100 g (3$^{1}/_{2}$ oz), cut into large pieces

Bring some water to the boil in a large pot. Place noodles in to cook for 2–3 minutes. Drain noodles and set aside.

In another pot, bring stock to the boil. Add chicken and cook until done. Remove chicken and leave to cool before shredding.

Add tofu and chye sim to stock. Allow stock to return to the boil, then remove from heat.

Divide noodles among 4 serving bowls. Top with shredded chicken, then ladle stock over with tofu and chye sim.

Garnish as desired. Serve immediately.

egg noodles with sauce

Cooked with generous portions of meat, seafood and vegetables, this makes a satisfying and well-balanced meal for tweens. (This dish is featured on the cover of this book.)

Dry egg noodles 4 bundles (150 g / 5$^1/_3$ oz)

Corn oil 2 Tbsp

Garlic 2 cloves, peeled and finely chopped

Chicken breast $^1/_2$ (110 g / 4 oz), skinned, thinly sliced

Prawns (shrimps) 12 (60 g / 2 oz), peeled and deveined

Squid 120 g (4$^1/_4$ oz), cleaned and cut into small pieces

Chye sim 50 g (1$^2/_3$ oz), cut into large pieces

Carrot $^1/_2$ (60 g / 2 oz), peeled and cut into thin strips

Homemade chicken stock (page 81) 2 cups (500 ml / 16 fl oz)

Rice wine 1 tsp

Black vinegar 1 Tbsp

Dark soy sauce 1 tsp

Salt and ground white pepper to taste

Corn flour (cornstarch) 1 Tbsp, mixed with 4 Tbsp water

Egg 1 (50 g / 1$^2/_3$ oz), lightly beaten

Sesame oil 2 tsp

Bring some water to the boil in a large pot. Place noodles in to cook for 2–3 minutes. Drain noodles and set aside.

Heat oil in a non-stick pan and fry garlic until fragrant. Add chicken, prawns and squid and cook for 2–3 minutes. Add vegetables and continue to stir-fry until just done. Add noodles and mix well.

In a separate pot, bring stock to the boil. Season with rice wine, vinegar, dark soy sauce and pepper, then thicken sauce with corn flour slurry. Taste and adjust with salt and pepper as needed. Slowly add beaten egg, stirring all the time. Remove from heat.

Divide noodles among 4 plates and ladle sauce over. Add sesame oil and garnish as desired. Serve immediately.

4 pax

10 min

12 min

nutrition fact
New studies have shown that dark soy sauce is 150 times more potent than vitamin C as an antioxidant, and may offer some disease protection. Gramme for gramme, soy sauce contains less sodium than salt, but it is still better to use it in small amounts when flavouring food.

Source: Riboflavin, Vitamin B$_{12}$
Good Source: Vitamin B$_6$, Copper, Niacin, Phosphorus
Excellent Source: Vitamin A, Vitamin K, Selenium

Nutritional Analysis (per serving)
Energy 360 kcal
Protein 30 g
Carbohydrate 33 g
Dietary fibre 2.0 g
Total fat 11.2 g
Saturated fat 2.5 g
Cholesterol 204 mg
Calcium 65 mg
Iron 2.4 mg

Some tweens hate vegetables, while others will eat up their greens without any fuss!

Vegetables are good for health and they are an essential part of a well-balanced diet. So, if you have young children, offer them vegetables early. Familiarity with vegetables fosters acceptance. Even if your children do not eat vegetables, don't stop offering it to them. Vary the types! Vary the cooking styles! Talk to them about the goodness of vegetables. Involve them in planting, buying, preparing and cooking vegetables. Eat vegetables in front of them. Persevere! Slowly, over time, your children will learn to accept vegetables.

Some parents go as far as camouflaging vegetables in food just to get some into their little ones. Tweens should be able to deal with vegetables like any adult, so resort to such drastic measures only if nothing else works. And if you do, continue to encourage your children to eat vegetables as a regular part of the diet.

Vegetables are naturally low in calories and sodium, and free of fat. They are at the same time, rich in fibre, vitamins and minerals. Colourful vegetables are chock-full of beneficial phytonutrients. So, brighten up your family's meals with vegetables! Buy vegetables of different colours and hues — green, red, yellow, orange, purple and white. Each colour pigment offers a promise of health and disease prevention.

To retain the nutrients in vegetables, wash, prepare and cut them just before cooking. Do not overcook vegetables as heat destroys fragile nutrients such as vitamin C. Steaming preserves nutrients in vegetables best. Stir-frying briefly with a little unsaturated oil also enables some phytonutrients and fat-soluble vitamins to become more available to the body. Encourage your tweens to eat some vegetables raw to enjoy the natural goodness of vegetables.

If you have to use frozen vegetables, take comfort in knowing that they are just as good, in their nutrient content, as many fresh vegetables, as they are blast-chilled soon after harvest.

Buy enough vegetables for the family. One serving of vegetables is made up of about a three-quarter cup, and tweens should have two servings daily. If each serving seems a little large for your children, serve vegetables in small portions throughout the day, even as snacks.

vital
veggies

Good Source: Vitamin K

Nutritional Analysis (per serving)

Energy 37 kcal	Saturated fat 0.3 g
Protein 4 g	Cholesterol 9 mg
Carbohydrate 3 g	Calcium 16 mg
Dietary fibre 1.3 g	Iron 1.5 mg
Total fat 1.4 g	

Baby asparagus and ham rolls

These leafless shoots are prized for their subtle taste and texture. Both slim and thick, and green and white spears of asparagus are widely available in supermarkets today. Here, they are lightly blanched to preserve the crunch and nutrients, then wrapped with a sheer sheet of very lean ham to tempt your tweens to try a bite.

Tender fresh baby asparagus spears 250 g (9 oz)
Honey baked ham or turkey ham 8 thin slices
Mayonnaise 2 tsp

Bring a pot of water to the boil and blanch asparagus spears for 1–2 minutes. Remove and drain, then quickly place into a bowl of cold water for 1 minute. Drain and set aside.

Divide asparagus into 8 portions. Place a slice of ham on a flat plate and arrange one portion of asparagus spears on one end of it. Squirt a little mayonnaise over, then roll up to keep it in place. Repeat until ingredients are used up.

Arrange on a serving plate and serve immediately.

nutrition fact

Asparagus is an excellent source of vitamin K, the B vitamin folate, vitamin C and vitamin A. It is also a good source of flavonoid phytonutrients.

cooking tip

Ham is rather high in sodium and fat. The best way to make a better choice is to look at the ham closely. Select a section with less visible fat and marbling. Ask the butcher to shave the ham thinly, so you can use just a teeny weeny bit to boost the flavour of plainer ingredients.

4 pax

10 min

20–25 min

flower power

This vibrant casserole combines two vegetables that many tweens adore — broccoli and cauliflower. Shaped like bouquets, these vegetables are bursting with vital nutrients. Served with a rich and creamy cheese sauce and a crispy-crunchy topping, this dish will be a hot favourite with tweens.

Homemade chicken stock (page 81) 2 cups (500 ml / 16 fl oz)

Broccoli 150 g (5$^1/_3$ oz), separated into florets

Cauliflower 200 g (7 oz), separated into florets

Low-fat milk powder 4 Tbsp

Corn flour (cornstarch) 3 Tbsp

Salt and ground black pepper to taste

Cheddar cheese 100 g (3$^1/_2$ oz), shredded

Breadcrumbs $^1/_4$ cup (20 g / $^2/_3$ oz)

Bring stock to the boil in a pot and blanch broccoli and cauliflower florets until three-quarters done. Remove and place florets in an ovenproof dish. Reserve stock.

Preheat oven to 250°C (475°F).

Mix together reserved stock, milk powder and corn flour in a heavy-based pan. Heat gently, stirring all the time. Season to taste with salt and pepper. When sauce is thick, stir in cheese, then pour over florets.

Sprinkle breadcrumbs over, then place in the oven and bake for 10–12 minutes, or until top is golden brown. Remove and serve immediately with bread or baked potatoes.

Good Source: Phosphorus, Calcium
Excellent Source: Vitamin K, Vitamin C

Nutritional Analysis (per serving)

Energy 160 kcal	Saturated fat 2.9 g
Protein 14 g	Cholesterol 14 mg
Carbohydrate 16 g	Calcium 376 mg
Dietary fibre 2.5 g	Iron 0.9 mg
Total fat 5.3 g	

nutrition fact

Bittergourd is rich in vitamins A, C and folate, as well as the minerals, magnesium, potassium and zinc. It is also high in fibre.

Excellent Source: Vitamin C

Nutritional Analysis (per serving)

Energy 62 kcal
Protein 3 g
Carbohydrate 3 g
Dietary fibre 2.1 g
Total fat 4.5 g
Saturated fat 1.0 g
Cholesterol 39 mg
Calcium 29 mg
Iron 0.6 mg

cooking tip

Select larger bittergourd fruit as it tends to be less bitter than small ones. Traditional cooking methods encourage soaking sliced bittergourd in salted water to reduce bitterness, but this will cause many water-soluble nutrients to be lost.

Bittergourd and egg scramble

Asian food traditions speak of the awesome goodness of bitter fruit and vegetables. Bittergourd is a good example of that! Many kids will rebel against the slightly bitter taste of this vegetable, but we have cooked it with eggs and anchovies to make it more palatable.

Bittergourd 1 medium (300 g / 11 oz)
Salt 1/2 tsp
Dried anchovies (*ikan bilis*) 1 Tbsp (20 g / 2/3 oz)
Corn oil 1 Tbsp
Garlic 2 cloves, peeled and minced
Egg 1 (50 g / 1 2/3 oz), well beaten

Cut bittergourd lengthwise in half, then scoop out pith and seeds. Slice thinly, then rub gently with 1/4 tsp salt. Set aside on a plate for 5–10 minutes.

Meanwhile, wash and drain dried anchovies. Lay them out on a microwaveable dish, then cook in the microwave oven on High for 2 minutes.

Heat oil in a wok and stir-fry garlic until fragrant. Drain bittergourd of any water, then add to wok and stir-fry for 5–8 minutes, or until cooked to taste.

Add egg and season with remaining salt. Mix well, then remove from heat. Dish out onto a serving plate.

Garnish with toasted dried anchovies. Serve hot with rice and other side dishes.

veggie fusion

This classic Chinese medley of vegetables is a great way to include woodear fungus in the diet. The vegetables are infused with a hint of garlic and a concert of traditional seasonings to make it a veritable delicacy.

Rice bran oil 1 Tbsp

Garlic 2 cloves, peeled and minced

Long cabbage 1/2 head (300 g / 11 oz), cut into pieces

Woodear fungus 5 g (1/6 oz), soaked to soften, thinly sliced in strips

Carrot 1/3 (70 g / 2 1/2 oz), peeled and thinly sliced

Baby corn 6 (50 g / 1 1/2 oz), sliced

Seasoning

Oyster sauce 2 Tbsp

Sesame oil 1 tsp

Corn flour (cornstarch) 1/2 tsp

Chinese cooking wine 1 tsp

Salt and ground white pepper to taste

Heat oil in a wok and stir-fry garlic until fragrant. Add cabbage and cook for 1 minute. Add woodear fungus, carrot and baby corn and continue to stir-fry until almost done. Takes 10–12 minutes.

In a separate bowl, combine seasoning ingredients, then add to wok, stirring until sauce is thick.

Dish out and serve hot with rice and other side dishes.

nutrition fact

Also known as black fungus, woodear is an economical way to achieve a lot of dietary fibre. It also is a good source of many B vitamins, iron, selenium and zinc. Just use a little to enhance a dish, as the reconstituted fungus expands quite a lot! Soak in water and wash well. The fungus has a slightly chewy texture and a bland taste that easily takes on the flavours of the seasonings it is cooked with.

Good Source: Vitamin C
Excellent Source: Vitamin A

Nutritional Analysis
(per serving)

Energy 68 kcal

Protein 1 g

Carbohydrate 5 g

Dietary fibre 1.2 g

Total fat 4.8 g

Saturated fat 0.8 g

Cholesterol 0 mg

Calcium 54 mg

Iron 0.4 mg

Good Source: Vitamin A

Nutritional Analysis (per serving)

Energy 88 kcal   Saturated fat 0 g
Protein 2 g   Cholesterol 0 mg
Carbohydrate 16 g   Calcium 25 mg
Dietary fibre 1.2 g   Iron 0.7 mg
Total fat 2.5 g

tangy asian salad

Raw vegetables retain more fragile nutrients like vitamin C, compared to cooked veggies, so train your tweens to eat some raw salads by serving it up as part of the regular family meal. Take care not to drown salads with loads of high fat dressing. This recipe combines a popular Asian sauce with lemon and honey for the dressing. Try it!

Cucumber 1/2 (200 g / 7 oz), peeled and grated

Tomato 1 medium (100 g / 3 1/2 oz), diced

Celery 1 stalk (50 g / 1 2/3 oz), diced

Carrot 1/8 (25 g / 1 oz), peeled and grated

Dressing

Fish sauce 2 Tbsp

Lemon juice 1 Tbsp

Honey 2 Tbsp

Garnish

Lettuce

Raisins 1 Tbsp

Cashew nuts 1 Tbsp, toasted and crushed

Combine ingredients for dressing and mix well. Set aside.

Toss together cucumber, tomato, celery and carrot. Drizzle dressing over and toss well.

Line a serving bowl with lettuce leaves. Arrange salad in bowl, then top with raisins and nuts. Serve.

nutrition fact

Celery is an excellent source of vitamin C and a very good source of dietary fibre, potassium, folate and vitamin B6. Its crunchy texture and unique flavour make it a valuable addition to salads and stir-fries.

4 pax

10 min

10 min

french Bean surprise

Made up with beans and carrots, and flavoured with toasted white bait, this dish will be a welcome side to complete your family meals. This recipe can be used to stir-fry many other vegetables. In East Asia, it is common to add a little lean meat, egg or fish to make the vegetable dish more delicious, and this may work with some tweens.

White bait 20 g (²/₃ oz), washed and drained
Olive oil 1 Tbsp
Garlic 3 cloves, peeled and minced
Firm tofu 200 g (7 oz) sliced
French beans 250 g (9 oz), sliced
Carrots 100 g (3¹/₂ oz), peeled and sliced
Salt and ground white pepper to taste

Lay white bait out on a microwave-safe dish, then cook in the microwave oven on High for 3 minutes, stirring once in between.

Meanwhile, heat oil in a wok and stir-fry garlic until fragrant. Add tofu and cook until brown. Add French beans and carrot slices and continue to stir-fry until tender but still crisp. Season to taste with salt and pepper. Dish out to a serving plate.

Top vegetables with toasted white bait. Serve hot with rice and other side dishes.

mushroom medley

This recipe celebrates the subtle flavours of fresh mushrooms by combining them with French beans and wolfberries. With the natural 'umami' taste evident, most tweens will take to this side dish without complaining.

Skinless chicken breast or drumstick 100 g (3$\frac{1}{2}$ oz) thinly sliced

Olive oil 1 Tbsp

Garlic 2 cloves, peeled and minced

French beans 15 (100 g / 3$\frac{1}{2}$ oz), thinly sliced

Fresh shiitake mushrooms 8 (30 g / 1 oz), cut into quarters

Canned button mushrooms 125 g (4$\frac{1}{2}$ oz), drained and cut into halves

Golden thread mushrooms 1 bundle (90 g / 3$\frac{1}{6}$ oz)

Chinese wolfberries 1 Tbsp

Marinade

Light soy sauce 1 tsp

Corn flour (cornstarch) 1 tsp

Chinese cooking wine 1 Tbsp

Seasoning

Light soy sauce 1 tsp

Corn flour (cornstarch) 1 tsp

Salt to taste

Combine ingredients for marinade in a bowl. Add chicken and mix well. Leave for 30 minutes.

In a separate bowl, combine seasoning ingredients and set aside.

Heat oil in a wok and stir-fry garlic until fragrant. Add marinated chicken and stir-fry for 2 minutes. Add French beans and mushrooms and stir-fry until vegetables are tender but still crisp.

Add Chinese wolfberries and prepared seasoning. Stir well and dish out. Serve hot with steamed rice and other side dishes.

4 pax

10 min
+ 30 min marinating

10 min

nutrition fact

Mushrooms contain more selenium than any other fruit or vegetable. Mushrooms are a good source of fibre as well as many B vitamins that have a role in releasing energy from carbohydrates, protein and fat.

Source: Pantothenic Acid, Copper, Selenium, Niacin
Good Source: Vitamin D

Nutritional Analysis
(per serving)

Energy 113 kcal
Protein 8 g
Carbohydrate 12 g
Dietary fibre 3.1 g
Total fat 4.5 g
Saturated fat 0.9 g
Cholesterol 19 mg
Calcium 20 mg
Iron 1.3 mg

4 pax

15 min

15 min

veggie parcels

Talk about serving up variety! This dish features five brightly-coloured vegetables, stir-fried lightly, then tucked into a steamed cabbage leaf. It makes a colourful side dish. The interesting presentation will attract adventurous tweens.

Cabbage leaves 4 large

Soy bean oil 1 Tbsp

Garlic paste 1 tsp

Chicken drumstick 1, skinned and finely sliced

Carrot $1/3$ (40 g / $1^{1}/_2$ oz), peeled and finely sliced

Baby corn 2, finely sliced

French beans 5, finely sliced

Mushroom sauce 1 Tbsp

Bean sprouts $1/2$ cup (50 g / $1^{2}/_3$ oz)

Water chestnut 1, peeled and finely chopped

Cut main vein from each cabbage leaf, then blanch leaves in hot water. Drain well and cool.

Heat oil in a non-stick pan and stir-fry garlic paste for 1 minute. Add chicken and stir-fry until done. Add sliced vegetables and season with mushroom sauce. Cook until tender but still crisp.

Add bean sprouts and water chestnut and cook lightly. Remove from heat and allow to cool.

Divide stir-fried vegetables into 4 portions and place one on each cabbage leaf. Roll up and secure with a toothpick. Steam rolls for 10 minutes and serve hot.

Good Source: Vitamin A

Nutritional Analysis (per serving)

Energy 68 kcal
Protein 5 g
Carbohydrate 4 g
Dietary fibre 1.2 g
Total fat 4.0 g

Saturated fat 0.8 g
Cholesterol 12 mg
Calcium 19 mg
Iron 0.5 mg

Source: Vitamin B$_6$, Manganese
Good Source: Vitamin A, Vitamin C
Excellent Source: Vitamin K

Nutritional Analysis (per serving)

Energy 234 kcal
Protein 8 g
Carbohydrate 25 g
Dietary fibre 2.8 g
Total fat 12.0 g

Saturated fat 4.4 g
Cholesterol 15 mg
Calcium 155 mg
Iron 1.7 mg

potato and spinach patties

The mashed potato conceals spinach and melted cheese in the heart of the patty, while the crispy bread coating provides an irresistible crunch. Packed with nutrients, these patties are really a must-have in your family's regular menu.

Olive oil 2 Tbsp

Onion 1 medium (100 g / 3^1/$_2$ oz)

Ginger paste 1 tsp

Garlic paste 1 tsp

Spinach leaves 60 g (2 oz), finely minced

Potatoes 2 medium (320 g / 11^1/$_3$ oz), boiled, peeled and mashed

Salt and ground white pepper to taste

Cheddar or cottage cheese 56 g (2 oz), cut into 8 small cubes

Egg white 35 g (1^1/$_4$ oz), lightly beaten

Breadcrumbs ^{1}/$_2$ cup (50 g / 1^2/$_3$ oz)

Heat 1 Tbsp olive oil in a wok and stir-fry onion until translucent. Add ginger and garlic pastes and stir-fry until fragrant. Add spinach leaves and stir-fry until soft. Add mashed potatoes and season with salt and pepper. Mix well and remove from heat. Divide into 8 portions and leave to cool slightly.

Take a portion of mashed potato mixture in your hand and flatten it using your fingers. Place a cube of cheese in the middle of mashed potato, then enclose and mould to form a patty of any shape you desire. Repeat with remaining ingredients.

Dip patties into egg white, then coat with breadcrumbs. Heat remaining oil in a frying pan and pan-fry patties on both sides until golden brown. Alternatively, if you prefer a more even colour for the patty, deep-fry them briefly until golden brown.

Serve hot as a snack or a side dish.

4 pax
(2 patties each)

12 min

20 min

nutrition fact

Potatoes, long misunderstood as being just a blob of carbohydrate, are really a nutritious food. They are a great source of fibre and vitamin C, vitamin B$_6$, and potassium. Most kids love potatoes any way it is cooked. Healthy ways to cook it are by roasting, boiling, steaming and grilling, with the skin on, of course!

cooking tip

Deep-frying increases the fat content of the patty. Here are some tips to do it right:

- Use a stable vegetable oil that withstands heat well. Peanut and canola oils are good for deep-frying.

- Heat oil well, but do not allow it to smoke.

- Ensure that the food you want to fry is as dry as possible.

- Deep-fry large pieces, as small pieces absorb more oil.

- Drain deep-fried food well, then dab away any excess oil with paper towels.

- Kids love deep-fried foods, so serve deep-fried foods to your tweens no more than two times a week. Keep the portion offered small as well!

4 pax

10 min

20 min

magenta magic

Brightly coloured vegetables are good for health, and here is one vegetable that will surely catch your eye. Steamed, then stir-fried, this beetroot dish will brighten any table, and your adventurous tweens may be happy to try it! Mix it up with a little rice to see the beautiful pink colour spread.

Fresh prawns 10 small (50 g / 1²/₃ oz), peeled and deveined

Light soy sauce 1 tsp

Beetroot 1 (200 g / 7 oz), peeled and cut into short sticks

Rice bran oil 1 Tbsp

Onion ¹/₂ medium (50 g / 1²/₃ oz), peeled and finely sliced

Garlic 2 cloves, peeled and minced

Dried prawns 1 Tbsp, washed and drained

Salt and ground white pepper to taste

Place prawns on a steaming plate and season with light soy sauce. Place in a steamer and steam for 7 minutes until tender. Remove and set aside. Place beetroot on another steaming plate and steam for about 10 minutes.

Heat oil in a wok and stir-fry onion and garlic until fragrant. Add dried prawns and cook for 1 minute. Add steamed beetroot and stir-fry for 1 minute until well mixed. Season with salt and pepper.

Dish out to a serving plate. Top with steamed prawns and serve hot with rice and other side dishes.

Good Source: Vitamin C, Iron, Folate, Dietary Fibre, Potassium

Nutritional Analysis (per serving)

Energy 82 kcal

Protein 6 g

Carbohydrate 7 g

Dietary fibre 1.6 g

Total fat 3.8 g

Saturated fat 0.7 g

Cholesterol 23 mg

Calcium 27 mg

Iron 1.2 mg

power Proteins

Tweens grow rapidly, and so they need sufficient protein to support the rapid growth that is characteristic of this period. Protein-rich foods are an important part of a well-balanced diet for tweens, but many tweens tend to include too much protein in their diet, as they love the taste of chicken, meat, fish, seafood and eggs!

Tweens should aim for two servings of protein a day. Ideally, one of the servings should be a plant-based protein like lentil or tofu. A serving of protein-rich food is described as one palm-sized piece of fish, chicken or lean meat, two small squares of tofu, or a three-quarter cup of cooked pulses.

Encourage your children to have one to two cups of milk each day. Yoghurt and cheese can also replace some milk in the diet as they provide protein and calcium as well.

To make a healthier choice, choose low-fat products and cook with less added fat. Select lean meat, skinless poultry and fish more often. Low-fat or non-fat dairy items should be the preferred choice.

When cooking, choose to steam, boil, bake, grill or stir-fry more often. Reserve deep-frying for special occasions, so your children will learn to appreciate the many other healthier cooking methods that you may use.

Source: Manganese
Good Source: Folate

Nutritional Analysis (per serving)

Energy 108 kcal   Saturated fat 0.3 g

Protein 7 g   Cholesterol 0 mg

Carbohydrate 17 g   Calcium 24 mg

Dietary fibre 7.9 g   Iron 2.1 mg

Total fat 1.5 g

lentil curry

Despite the name, this is not a spicy dish! This traditional Indian dish is a wonderful way to include a variety of dried lentils to the diet. Cooked with a variety of herbs and spices, the plain lentils take on a truly delicious flavour. Serve with rice or chapattis and vegetables to complete the meal. .

Water 2 cups (500ml / 16 fl oz)

Split green lentils 1/2 cup (100 g / 3 1/2 oz), washed

Onion 1/2 medium (50 g / 1 2/3 oz), peeled and finely sliced

Garlic 2 cloves, peeled and finely minced

Ginger 0.5-cm (1/4-in) knob, peeled and finely minced

Cooking oil 1 tsp

Ground turmeric 1/2 tsp

Green chilli (optional) 1/2, sliced

Tomato 1 medium (100 g / 3 1/2 oz), chopped

Salt to taste

Lemon juice to taste

Coriander leaves (cilantro) 1 sprig

Bring water to the boil in a pot. Add lentils, onion, garlic, ginger and oil. Lower heat and cook until lentils are soft. Takes about 20 minutes.

Add turmeric, green chili and tomato. When tomato is soft, season with salt and lemon juice.

Remove from heat and top with coriander leaves. Dish out and serve hot.

nutrition fact

Lentils are a rich source of protein. Enjoy them with a grain food to help complete the protein profile. Low in saturated fat and completely free of cholesterol, lentils are also a good source of iron, folate and soluble fibre — the heart-friendly type that helps maintain a healthy cholesterol level.

cooking tip

Split lentils cook faster than whole dried beans. If you have never eaten lentils before, you may want to start with just a little. Some sensitive individuals experience an episode of flatulence when they eat these fibre-rich plant proteins.

4 pax

10 min

25 min

fish pie

Kids who do not eat fish slices can be tempted to try this out. Somehow, the interesting combination of fish flakes and vegetables gently folded into a tangy, light mayonnaise is not as intimidating as a piece of fish with bone.

Potato 1 medium (220 g / 8 oz)
Spanish mackerel fillet 350 g (12 oz), cut into cubes
Celery 1/2 stalk (50 g / 1²/₃ oz), finely minced
Carrot 1/2 (36 g / 1¹/₂ oz), peeled and grated
Low-fat mayonnaise 6 Tbsp
Butter 1 tsp
Salt and ground white pepper to taste

Bring a small pot of water to the boil and cook potato with skin on until tender.

Bring another small pot of water to the boil and cook fish. Drain and cool, then gently flake fish. Mix with celery, carrot and low-fat mayonnaise. Portion mixture into 4 small pie dishes.

Peel, then mash potato. Flavour with butter, salt and pepper, then spoon into a piping bag with a large nozzle. Pipe over fish mixture in pie dishes, then place under the grill to brown the top.

Serve immediately with a side salad and bread roll.

cooking tip
Mackerel is widely available. Ask the fishmonger to fillet the fish and remove the skin for you.

chawanmushi

This quick and easy Japanese dish presents a savoury egg custard that most tweens will love. Vary the toppings to create varieties that are uniquely your own family recipe.

Eggs 2 (100 g / $3^1/_2$ oz)

Homemade chicken stock (page 81) $^1/_2$ cup (125 ml / 4 fl oz)

Salt and ground white pepper to taste

Dried Chinese mushroom 1, soaked to soften, stem removed and thinly sliced

Prawns (shrimps) 4 small (20 g / $^2/_3$ oz), peeled and halved

Crabstick 1 (20 g / $^2/_3$ oz), cut into 4 short lengths

Lightly beat eggs, then mix with chicken stock. Season with salt and pepper. Strain mixture.

Pour mixture into 4 small bowls with lids. Cover bowls and place in a steamer. Steam for 5 minutes.

Remove covers and top custard with sliced mushrooms, prawns and crabstick. Replace lids and steam for another 5 minutes.

Remove from steamer and serve warm.

4 pax

8 min

10 min

Nutritional Analysis (per serving)

Energy 47 kcal
Protein 5 g
Carbohydrate 2 g
Dietary fibre 0.1 g
Total fat 2.4 g
Saturated fat 0.7 g
Cholesterol 101 mg
Calcium 15 mg
Iron 0.6 mg

nutrition fact
Prawns are a good source of protein, selenium and vitamin D. They are low in fat and saturated fat, and contain heart-healthy unsaturated fat, especially Omega-3. Despite the higher cholesterol content, prawns can be used in small portions to add variety and colour to meals.

savoury tomato cups

These little tomato cups filled with a cheese-flavoured egg custard and topped with prawns will be a hit with many tweens. Serve it as a side dish or along with breakfast to add colour and a whole host of nutrients to the meal.

Tomatoes 4 (400 g / 14^1/$_3$ oz)

Eggs 2 (100 g / 3^1/$_2$ oz)

Prawns (shrimps) 4 large (80 g / 2^4/$_5$ oz), peeled, deveined and halved

Grated Cheddar cheese 2 Tbsp

Coriander leaves (cilantro) 1 Tbsp, minced

Salt and ground white pepper to taste

Preheat oven to 180°C (350°F).

Halve each tomato across. Cut decoratively if desired. Remove soft centres with a spoon. Place on a baking tray. If tomato cups do not sit flat, support them with aluminium foil.

Beat eggs, then add prawns, cheese, coriander leaves, salt and pepper. Mix well, then pour into tomato halves. Carefully place tomatoes in the oven for 20–25 minutes until egg mixture is set and prawns are cooked.

Remove from oven and garnish as desired. Serve warm.

Good Source: Vitamin A, Vitamin C, Selenium

Nutritional Analysis (per serving)

Energy 97 kcal   Saturated fat 2.3 g

Protein 9 g   Cholesterol 117 mg

Carbohydrate 4 g   Calcium 84 mg

Dietary fibre 1.2 g   Iron 1.1 mg

Total fat 4.9 g

Beef Moussaka

This Greek-inspired casserole dish of aubergine and minced beef will be a favourite with meat-loving tweens.

Aubergine (eggplant) 1 medium (225 g / 8 oz), thinly sliced
Olive oil 2 Tbsp
Onion 1/2 medium (50 g /1²/₃ oz), peeled and minced
Garlic 1 clove, peeled and minced
Tomato 1 large (150 g / 5¹/₃ oz), chopped
Tomato purée 1¹/₂ Tbsp
Mixed oregano and basil ¹/₈ tsp
Mixed ground nutmeg and cinnamon ¹/₈ tsp
Lean minced beef 250 g (9 oz)
Butter ¹/₂ Tbsp
Plain (all-purpose) flour 1¹/₂ Tbsp
Low-fat milk ¹/₂ cup (125 ml / 4 fl oz)
Cheddar cheese 30 g (1 oz)

Slice aubergine just before baking to prevent slices from browning. Brush some oil on a baking tray and arrange aubergine slices in a layer on tray. Place under a hot grill until lightly browned. Turn slices over, brush lightly with oil, then continue to grill until brown.

Heat oil in a non-stick pan. Stir-fry onion and garlic until fragrant. Add tomato, purée, herbs and spices and cook until tomato is soft. Add beef and cook until done and dry. Season to taste. Set aside.

Melt butter in a heavy-based pan. Add flour and cook for 1 minute, stirring all the time. Add milk and continue stirring until sauce starts to thicken. Add half the cheese and stir well. Remove from heat.

Preheat oven to 200°C (400°F).

Brush a baking dish lightly with oil and start layering. Begin with a layer of auberine slices, then half the meat sauce, another layer of aubergine, remaining meat sauce and finishing with aubergine. Pour white sauce over and sprinkle with remaining cheese.

Place in the oven and bake for 1 hour. Remove from oven and leave to stand for a few minutes before cutting to serve.

lamb stew

In this recipe, the lamb is gently stewed to allows its flavour to permeate the other ingredients, making the dish absolutely delicious. Serve with bread, mashed potatoes or rice.

Lean lamb 400 g (14$^{1}/_{3}$ oz), cut into cubes

Onions 2 (240 g / 8$^{1}/_{2}$ oz), peeled and cut into cubes

Ginger paste 1 tsp

Garlic paste 1 tsp

Cinnamon stick 2.5-cm (1-in)

Cloves 2

Salt 1 tsp

Ground black pepper $^{1}/_{2}$ tsp

Olive oil 1 Tbsp

Potato 1 medium (210 g / 7$^{1}/_{2}$ oz), peeled and cut into cubes

Carrot 1 (150 g / 5$^{1}/_{3}$ oz), peeled and cut into cubes

Celery 1 stalk (140 g / 5 oz), cut into cubes

Place lamb, 1 onion, ginger, garlic, cinnamon, cloves, salt and pepper in a pressure cooker and place over high heat. Allow steam to rise through the vent (about 8–10 minutes), then place the weight and cook for another 10 minutes. Allow to cool.

Alternatively, place ingredients in a slow-cooker until lamb is soft and tender. Takes about 3 hours.

Heat oil in a pan. Add remaining onion, potato and carrot and stir-fry for 2–3 minutes. Add lamb and allow vegetables to cook until tender.

Add celery and cook for another 2–3 minutes. Dish out and serve hot.

4 pax

10 min

20 min

nutrition fact

Lamb is another red meat that is rich in protein. Select lean cuts to reduce fat, saturated fat and cholesterol content. Lamb is also a great source of iron, zinc and vitamin B$_{12}$.

Source: Riboflavin, Zinc, Vitamin K, Vitamin B$_6$
Good Source: Vitamin B$_{12}$, Vitamin C, Niacin, Phosphorus, Selenium
Excellent Source: Vitamin A

Nutritional Analysis
(per serving)
Energy 260 kcal
Protein 23 g
Carbohydrate 20 g
Dietary fibre 3.6 g
Total fat 9.6 g
Saturated fat 2.9 g
Cholesterol 66 mg
Calcium 58 mg
Iron 2.6 mg

4 pax

10 min

20 min

herb-crusted cod fish

Cod is a mild-tasting, low-fat fish. Packing it with local herbs and gently baking it, allows the flavours and aroma to penetrate the delicate flesh.

Lemon grass 4 g (¹/₆ oz), finely minced
Spring onion (scallion) 4 g (¹/₆ oz), finely minced
Coriander leaves (cilantro) 4 g (¹/₆ oz), finely minced
Black peppercorns ¹/₂ tsp, finely crushed
Sea salt ¹/₄ tsp, finely crushed
Cod fish fillets 4, each about 120 g (4¹/₄ oz)
Olive oil

Preheat oven to 200°C (400°F).

Mix herbs with pepper and salt on a plate. Rub fish fillets with a little olive oil then, coat with seasoned herbs.

Heat some oil in a pan. Pan-fry fish until lightly brown on both sides, then gently transfer to a baking tray lined with non-stick baking paper.

Bake for 10 minutes until fish is cooked. Remove and serve hot.

tangy salmon cake

In this recipe, fish is blended with cold water, then steamed to make a pretty pink cake. Served with a tasty honey-lemon sauce, it will be a favourite on your family's dining table.

White fish fillet (mackerel or dory) 200 g (7 oz), cut into cubes

Salmon fillet 120 g (4$\frac{1}{4}$ oz), cut into cubes

Ice cold water $\frac{1}{2}$ cup (125 ml / 4 fl oz)

Salt 1 tsp

Ground white pepper 1 tsp

Corn flour (cornstarch) 1$\frac{1}{2}$ Tbsp

Coriander leaves (cilantro) 10 g ($\frac{1}{3}$ oz), finely chopped

Spring onion (scallion) 10 g ($\frac{1}{3}$ oz), finely chopped

Sauce

Canola oil 1 Tbsp

Ginger 5 g ($\frac{1}{6}$ oz), peeled and thinly sliced

Honey 1 Tbsp

Sugar $\frac{1}{2}$ tsp

Lemon juice 2 Tbsp

Salt $\frac{1}{4}$ tsp

Light soy sauce $\frac{1}{2}$ tsp

Sesame oil $\frac{1}{2}$ tsp

Cooking wine, 1 tsp

Water 4 Tbsp

Corn flour (cornstarch) 1 tsp

Place fish and cold water in a blender and blend into a smooth paste. Take care not to allow mixture to get hot. Remove from blender and mix in salt, pepper, corn flour, coriander and spring onion.

Spoon paste onto a well oiled steaming plate, pressing it down so cake takes the shape of plate. Steam for 10 minutes until done. Leave to cool.

Meanwhile prepare sauce. Heat oil in a pan and fry ginger until golden brown. Combine remaining ingredients for sauce and add to pan. Stir over low heat until sauce is thick. Pour over fish cake. Slice and serve.

4 pax

10 min

25 min

nutrition fact

Salmon is a great source of protein. It is naturally high in thiamin, niacin and vitamins B$_6$ and B$_{12}$ and selenium. It also provides the heart-friendly, unsaturated Omega-3 fat.

Source: Vitamin B$_{12}$, Vitamin B$_6$, Niacin, Phosphorus
Good Source: Selenium

Nutritional Analysis
(per serving)

Energy 178 kcal

Protein 16 g

Carbohydrate 9 g

Dietary fibre 0.4 g

Total fat 8.5 g

Saturated fat 1.5 g

Cholesterol 48 mg

Calcium 24 mg

Iron 0.7 mg

cooking tip

Many tweens are put off by the "fishy" smell of fish. To make the experience more pleasant, buy fresh fish and wash it well. Use herbs and tangy sauces to mask any smells. Keep to the cooking time specified in the recipe, as overcooking fish makes the smell more pungent.

Source: Vitamin B$_6$, Thiamin
Good Source: Phosphorus, Vitamin C

Nutritional Analysis (per serving)

Energy 325 kcal	Saturated fat 3.0 g
Protein 21 g	Cholesterol 48 mg
Carbohydrate 25 g	Calcium 33 mg
Dietary fibre 2.7 g	Iron 1.6 mg
Total fat 16.0 g	

fish fingers and fries

Most kids love fish fingers and fries. Pan-fry the fish and bake the fries for a healthier version. However, if your tween's diet is already low in fat, you can offer this dish the classic way — deep-fried.

Potatoes 2 medium (420 g / 14⁴/₅ oz)

Dory fish fillet 350 g (12 oz), cut into fingers

Garlic paste ¹/₂ tsp

Ginger paste ¹/₂ tsp

Lemon juice ¹/₂ tsp

Salt and ground white pepper to taste

Egg white 1, lightly beaten

Breadcrumbs ³/₄ cup (20 g / ²/₃ oz)

Soy bean oil 3 Tbsp

Wash potatoes and peel potatoes if desired. Cut into fingers and place in a steamer to steam for 10 minutes.

Meanwhile, line 2 baking trays with non-stick baking paper. Preheat oven to 200°C (400°F) when potatoes are almost ready.

Arrange steamed potato fingers on a prepared baking tray. Bake for 10 minutes until golden brown.

Season fish with garlic, ginger, lemon juice, salt and pepper. Dip into egg white and coat with breadcrumbs.

Heat oil in a frying pan and pan-fry fish fillets to brown the outside. Remove from pan and place on a prepared baking tray. Bake for 10 minutes.

Serve fish fingers with fries.

nutrition fact

Egg white is a great source of protein and free of cholesterol. In this recipe, only the egg white is used to keep the cholesterol content low.

4 pax

10 min

10 min

nutrition fact

Garbanzo beans are a good source of protein and folate, and are high in fibre, especially the soluble kind. They are also low in fat and saturated fat and free of cholesterol.

cooking tip

Whole dried garbanzo beans are available from Indian grocery stores. The cooked, canned version is more widely available at supermarkets. Canned garbanzo beans are convenient as they shorten the preparation and cooking times tremendously. Drain the canned beans well to reduce the sodium content.

savoury Beans

This is a tasty way to include whole dried beans into your tween's diet. Cooked with a savoury tomato-based sauce, this protein-rich dish can be enjoyed with rice or bread. Garbanzo beans are also known as chickpeas.

Corn oil 2 Tbsp

Onion 1 medium (100 g / 3^1/$_2$ oz), peeled and thinly sliced

Ginger 1 tsp, finely ground

Garlic 1 tsp, finely ground

Curry powder (optional) 1 tsp

Tomato 1 medium (110 g / 4 oz), chopped

Tomato purée 1 Tbsp

Canned garbanzo beans 1 can (250 g / 9 oz), drained

Salt to taste

Heat oil in a frying pan and stir-fry onion, ginger and garlic until fragrant. Add curry powder, tomato and purée and cook for another 2 minutes.

Add garbanzo beans and mix well to heat through. Season with salt.

Dish out and serve hot with rice or bread.

Source: Iron, Manganese, Magnesium,
Copper, Panthothenic Acid
Good Source: Vitamin A, Vitamin D, Vitamin B$_6$,
Phosphorus, Thiamin
Excellent Source: Vitamin B$_{12}$, Vitamin C,
Niacin, Selenium

Nutritional Analysis (per serving)

Energy 330 kcal	Saturated fat 3.0 g
Protein 41 g	Cholesterol 211 mg
Carbohydrate 6 g	Calcium 75 mg
Dietary fibre 0.8 g	Iron 3.2 mg
Total fat 15.0 g	

seafood on skewers

Seafood on skewers offers a healthier way to prepare delicate fish and prawns. Take care not to burn the food too much.

Mackerel fillet 400 g (14^1/$_3$ oz)

Prawns (shrimps) 400 g (14^1/$_3$ oz), peeled and deveined

Pumpkin 60 g (2 oz), cut into cubes

Pineapple 60 g (2 oz), cut into cubes

Green capsicum (bell pepper) 100 g (3^1/$_2$ oz), cut into cubes

Marinade

Olive oil 2 Tbsp

Garlic paste ^{1}/$_2$ tsp

Ginger paste ^{1}/$_2$ tsp

Light soy sauce 1 Tbsp

Lemon juice 2 tsp

Combine ingredients for marinade in a bowl. Add mackerel and prawns and mix well. Cover and refrigerate for 20 minutes.

Place pumpkin cubes in a steamer and steam for 5–8 minutes until pumpkin is tender, but still firm.

Preheat oven to 210°C (410°F).

Using bamboo skewers, thread fish, prawns, pineapple, steamed pumpkin and capsicum alternately. Place on a baking tray lined with non-stick baking paper.

Place in the oven for 10 minutes. Turn skewers over once or twice while cooking.

Serve hot with rice.

4 pax

10 min
+ 20 min marinating

10 min

nutrition fact

Olive oil is unsaturated oil that is rich in monounsaturates. Extra virgin olive oil is made from the first 'pressing' of crushed olives. It is richer in beneficial polyphenol antioxidants than the more refined version that is generically called olive oil.

4 pax

10 min
+ 20–30 min marinating

20 min

coriander chicken

In this dish, the aroma of fresh coriander permeates the chicken meat, which is slowly dry-roasted to achieve the golden brown colour. Tweens will easily take to this tasty dish as a replacement for deep-fried chicken.

Chicken drumsticks 8 (960 g / 2 lb 2 oz), skinned

Ginger paste 1 tsp

Garlic paste 1 tsp

Coriander leaves (cilantro) 20 g (²/₃ oz), finely chopped

Lemon juice 1 tsp

Salt and ground black pepper to taste

Corn oil 2 Tbsp

Marinate chicken drumsticks with ginger, garlic, coriander, lemon juice, salt and pepper. Cover and refrigerate for 20–30 minutes.

Heat oil in a wok. Gently place marinated chicken into wok over high heat so chicken browns. Turn chicken over to brown all sides. Lower heat and allow chicken to cook thoroughly.

Test if chicken is cooked by inserting a skewer into the thickest part of chicken. Juices should run clear.

Dish out and serve.

Source: Vitamin C
Good Source: Vitamin K, Riboflavin,
Vitamin B₆, Pantothenic Acid,
Zinc, Phosphorus, Selenium
Excellent Source: Niacin

Nutritional Analysis (per serving)

Energy 350 kcal	Saturated fat 3.5 g
Protein 50 g	Cholesterol 185 mg
Carbohydrate 0.9 g	Calcium 34 mg
Dietary fibre 0.3 g	Iron 2.7 mg
Total fat 15.0 g	

Source: Riboflavin, Niacin, Phosphorus, Vitamin A
Good Source: Vitamin B₆, Selenium
Excellent Source: Thiamin

Nutritional Analysis (per serving)

Energy 166 kcal	Saturated fat 1.2 g
Protein 22 g	Cholestero 65 mg
Carbohydrate 11 g	Calcium 17 mg
Dietary fibre 0.9 g	Iron 1.5 mg
Total fat 3.5 g	

pork and veggie rolls

Quick and simple, this recipe turns out a delicately flavoured roll that is chock-full of vegetables. It makes an excellent replacement for processed sausages.

Lean minced pork 400 g (14^1/$_3$ oz)

Onion ^{1}/$_2$ small (40 g /1^1/$_2$ oz), peeled and finely minced

Garlic 2 cloves, peeled and finely minced

Water chestnuts 2 (30 g / 1 oz), peeled and finely minced

Raisins 2 Tbsp, minced

Carrot ^{1}/$_8$ (25 g / 1 oz), peeled and finely minced

Coriander leaves (cilantro) 5 g (^{1}/$_6$ oz), finely minced

Salt and ground white pepper to taste

Corn flour (cornstarch) 2 Tbsp

Sesame oil a dash

Combine all ingredients in a mixing bowl and mix well.

Divide into 4 portions and shape each portion into a long roll.

Wrap in aluminium foil and place in a steamer. Steam for 25 minutes until meat is cooked.

Unwrap, slice and serve. Alternatively, pan-fry the steamed rolls until lightly browned before slicing to serve.

nutrition fact

In spite of its name, water chestnut is not a nut, but a vegetable. It is naturally low in calories and free of fat. Water chestnuts are also a great source of fibre.

4 pax

15 min

25 min

nutrition fact
Curry powder is made from a blend of many herbs and spices, with a key ingredient being turmeric, also called curcumin. Turmeric is a powerful antioxidant that may prevent some chronic diseases. While there is currently no conclusion about the health benefits of curry powder, it is still a tasty option to include in your family's dining menu.

mild chicken curry

Curry originated from Indian food culture, but it is now enjoyed all over the world. Unlike popular belief, not all curries are hot and spicy. This mild curry makes a gentle introduction for your tweens to the wonderful world of herbs and spices.

Corn oil 2 Tbsp

Onion 1 medium (110 g / 4 oz), peeled and thinly sliced

Ginger paste 1 tsp

Garlic paste 1 tsp

Chicken curry powder 1 Tbsp

Tomato 1 medium (120 g / $4^{1}/_{4}$ oz), cut into wedges

Baby potatoes 200 g (7 oz), washed and scrubbed clean; halved or left whole

Chicken breasts 2 (470 g / 1 lb $^{2}/_{3}$ oz), skin and fat removed, cut into cubes

Water $^{1}/_{2}$ cup (125 ml / 4 fl oz)

Salt to taste

Low-fat evaporated milk $^{1}/_{2}$ cup (125 ml / 4 fl oz)

Heat oil in a pan and fry onion until golden brown. Add ginger and garlic and stir-fry until fragrant but not brown.

Mix curry powder with 2 Tbsp water into a paste and add to pan. Cook for 2–3 minutes, stirring well all the time.

Add tomato, potatoes and chicken cubes. Continue to cook for another 2–3 minutes, then add water and season with salt.

Cook until chicken is well done. Remove from heat and stir in evaporated milk.

Dish out and serve hot with rice.

Source: Magnesium
Good Source: Vitamin B$_6$, Vitamin C,
Phosphorus, Selenium
Excellent Source: Niacin

Nutritional Analysis (per serving)

Energy 309 kcal	Saturated fat 2.5 g
Protein 32 g	Cholesterol 70 mg
Carbohydrate 18 g	Calcium 134 mg
Dietary fibre 2.5 g	Iron 2.0 mg
Total fat 12.1 g	

delicious desserts

Eating is enjoyed simply because it is pure pleasure. And, enjoying food is not wrong as long as one has control over the amount eaten.

Desserts, sweet and delicious, are truly the highlight of formal meals. Many traditional favourites are high in fat and sugar, so train your tweens to appreciate the milder and lighter flavours of healthier desserts.

You can even use a dessert to pack in many nutrients into your tween's diet. Substitute ingredients to reduce fat, sugar and calories. Add fruit, nuts and low-fat dairy products to increase the nutrient density of each mouthful. In spite of these suggestions, keep desserts as an occasional treat and not a staple in the diet. Also, keep the serving portions small, so your tweens can maintain a healthy weight.

Nutritional Analysis (per serving)

Energy 99 kcal   Saturated fat 0.5 g
Protein 8 g   Cholesterol 0 mg
Carbohydrate 13 g   Calcium 37 mg
Dietary fibre 0.9 g   Iron 1.2 mg
Total fat 2.4 g

choco soy pudding

Smooth and light like a soufflé, this pudding is yummy and easy to make. Serve it with a light chocolate sauce and fresh fruit.

Gelatine powder 1 Tbsp

Warm water 5 Tbsp (75 ml / $2^1/_2$ fl oz)

Silken tofu 300 g (11 oz)

Cocoa powder 2 Tbsp

Brown sugar 4 Tbsp

Egg whites 2 (66 g / $2^1/_3$ oz)

Stir gelatine into warm water and set aside until well soaked.

Place tofu, cocoa powder, sugar and gelatine into a mixing bowl and blend with a hand-held blender until mixture is smooth. Refrigerate for 1 hour to set partially.

Whip egg whites until white and stiff. Fold gently into the chilled, setting pudding until well mixed.

Pour pudding into 4 small bowls or cups. Return to the refrigerator to chill and set completely. Takes 2–3 hours. Serve cold.

4 pax (2 skewers each)

10 min

fruit kebabs

Fruit are nature's most delicious desserts. Naturally rich in fibre, low in calories, free of fat, and full of many vital vitamins and minerals, these wonderful sweet delicacies are great value for calories.

Rock melon 160 g (5^2/$_3$ oz), chilled
Honeydew melon 160 g (5^2/$_3$ oz), chilled
Kiwi fruit 160 g (5^2/$_3$ oz), chilled
Strawberries 160 g (5^2/$_3$ oz), chilled
Jack fruit 160 g (5^2/$_3$ oz), chilled
Chocolate sauce 2 Tbsp, chilled

Cut skin off melons. Peel kiwi fruit. Hull strawberrie.

Cut fruit into small pieces using a knife or a small scoop. Use bamboo skewers to thread fruit. Make 8 skewers in all.

Drizzle skewers with chocolate sauce before serving.

nutrition fact

Melons are a good source of potassium, vitamin B$_6$ and folate. Rockmelon is also rich in niacin, while honeydew provides vitamin C.

Strawberries are a great source of vitamin C, folate, potassium and dietary fibre. They are also excellent sources of the phytonutrients, anthocyanin and ellagic acid, known to protect against heart disease.

Good Source: Vitamin A
Excellent Source: Vitamin C

Nutritional Analysis (per serving)

Energy 130 kcal	Saturated fat 0.1 g
Protein 2 g	Cholesterol 0 mg
Carbohydrate 32 g	Calcium 38 mg
Dietary fibre 3.7 g	Iron 0.9 mg
Total fat 0.7 g	

nutrition fact

Mangoes are a heavenly tropical fruit. Its intense sweetness and unique flavour and aroma are irresistible. Mangoes are a great source of vitamins C, A and B₆. They are also naturally rich in fibre.

Excellent Source:
Vitamin C

**Nutritional Analysis
(per serving)**
Energy 112 kcal
Protein 4 g
Carbohydrate 21 g
Dietary fibre 2 g
Total fat 2.2 g
Saturated fat 0.6 g
Cholesterol 4 mg
Calcium 88 mg
Iron 0.4 mg

fruity macaroni energiser

This dessert really is a powerhouse of energy for active kids. Combining fresh fruit with cooked pasta makes it rich in carbohydrates, both sugar and starch. Tweens will love the sweet taste and smooth consistency of this dish..

Macaroni 1/4 cup (35 g / 1 1/4 oz)

Ripe mango 1/4 cup (50 g / 1 2/3 oz), peeled and cut into cubes

Papaya 1/4 cup (50 g / 1 2/3 oz), peeled and cut into cubes

Strawberries 1/4 cup (50 g / 1 2/3 oz), hulled and cut into cubes

Red apples 1/4 cup (50 g / 1 2/3 oz), cored and cut into cubes

Green kiwi fruit 1/4 cup (50 g / 1 2/3 oz), peeled and cut into cubes

Raisins 1 Tbsp

Low-fat yoghurt 2/3 cup (160 ml / 7 1/2 fl oz)

Low-fat mayonnaise 1 Tbsp

Honey (optional) 1 Tbsp

Bring a large pot of water to the boil and cook macaroni for 8 minutes. Drain and set aside to cool.

When cool, place macaroni in a large bowl and mix with fruit cubes, raisins, yoghurt, mayonnaise and honey.

Refrigerate until chilled before serving. Takes about 3 hours.

mango sago surprise

Replacing the coconut milk used in the traditional recipe with low-fat evaporated milk transforms this Asian dessert into a lower calorie dish that is more nutrient-dense. This recipe is also a particularly good source of calcium, the nutrient that supports the building of strong bones and teeth.

Chopped palm sugar 4 Tbsp
Pearl sago 80 g (2⁴/₅ oz)
Low-fat evaporated milk 1 cup (250 ml / 8 fl oz)
Ice cubes 1 cup
Ripe mango 1 (500 g / 1 lb 1¹/₂ oz), peeled, stoned and cut into cubes

Place palm sugar in a small saucepan with 2–3 Tbsp water to dissolve sugar. Place over low heat and stir to dissolve. Set aside.

Bring a pot of water to the boil. Add sago and continue boiling until sago is transparent. Drain sago, then rinse with cold water. Drain again and set aside.

In a large bowl, combine evaporated milk, ice cubes, sago and mango cubes. Serve immediately, with palm sugar syrup on the side.

4 pax

10 min

10 min

Source: Vitamin A, Calcium
Excellent Source: Vitamin C

Nutritional Analysis
(per serving)
Energy 240 kcal
Protein 6 g
Carbohydrate 56 g
Dietary fibre 2.3 g
Total fat 0.5 g
Saturated fat 0.2 g
Cholesterol 2.7 mg
Calcium 218 mg
Iron 0.8 mg

cooking tip
When cooking sago, remember to start with a lot of water to prevent sticking. Add the sago to boiling water to prevent the sago from dissolving. Stir constantly to prevent lumping and burning. If mango is not in season, replace with rockmelon or honeydew.

Nutritional Analysis (per serving)

Energy 82 kcal

Protein 0 g

Carbohydrate 21 g

Dietary fibre 2 g

Total fat 0.2 g

Saturated fat 0 g

Cholesterol 0 mg

Calcium 7 mg

Iron 0.8 mg

juicy jellies

Most children love cool, sweet jellies. This recipe, made entirely of fruit juice and fresh fruit is free of added sugar. The delicate gel set achieved with konnyaku is absolutely tender, yet firm.

Konnyaku jelly powder 5 g ($^1/_6$ oz)
Freshly extracted apple juice 2 cups (500 ml / 16 fl oz)
Longans 60 g (2 oz), peeled, stoned and cut into cubes
Ripe mango 60 g (2 oz) peeled, stoned and cut into cubes

Combine konnyaku powder with apple juice in a saucepan and bring to the boil, stirring to dissolve konnyaku. Continue to boil for 5 more minutes until bubbles disappear. Transfer to a pouring jug.

Prepare jelly moulds. Place equal portions of longan and mango cubes in moulds, then pour in konnyaku. Set aside to cool before refrigerating to chill and set. Takes about 3 hours.

Remove jellies from moulds and serve cold as a snack or dessert.

4 pax

10 min

15 min
+ 3 hr chilling

nutrition fact
Konnyaku is low in calories and high in fibre.

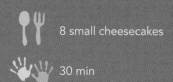

lemon cheesecake

Absolutely delicious, this tangy low-fat variation of cheesecake is high in protein and calcium. Gently chilled to set with gelatine, this dessert requires no baking.

Gelatine powder 2 Tbsp

Water 1/4 cup (60 ml / 2 fl oz)

Light digestive biscuits 100 g (3 1/2 oz)

Butter 50 g (1 2/3 oz), melted and cooled

Low-fat cream cheese 125 g (4 1/2 oz)

Low-fat cottage cheese 75 g (2 1/3 oz)

Low-fat evaporated milk 100 ml (3 1/3 fl oz)

Sugar 5 Tbsp

Lemon juice 2 Tbsp

Grated lemon zest 1 Tbsp

Prepare 8 small ring cutters, each about 8-cm (3-in) wide. Wrap base with aluminium foil.

Mix gelatine with water and leave to soak for 20 minutes.

Crush digestive biscuits until fine, then add butter and mix to form a rough crumble. Press crumble into prepared ring cutters to form a base about 1-cm (1/2-in) deep.

Using a blender, blend cream cheese, cottage cheese, evaporated milk, sugar, lemon juice and gelatine mixture until smooth and well mixed. Stir in lemon rind.

Pour filling onto crumble bases placed on a tray. Cover with aluminium foil or plastic wrap. Refrigerate to chill and set. Takes about 3 hours.

When ready to serve, remove cover and aluminium foil. Gently ease cheesecake from mould. Garnish with fresh fruit and serve.

Nutritional Analysis (per cheesecake)

Energy 178 kcal
Protein 4 g
Carbohydrate 9 g
Dietary fibre 0.5 g
Total fat 9.9 g

Saturated fat 4.9 g
Cholesterol 23 mg
Calcium 67 mg
Iron 0.4 mg

Nutritional Analysis (per lolly)

Energy 56 kcal	Saturated fat 0.2 g
Protein 1 g	Cholesterol 1 mg
Carbohydrate 13 g	Calcium 37 mg
Dietary fibre 1.2 g	Iron 0.2 mg
Total fat 0.5 g	

sunshine lollies

Hot summer days and chilled lollies simply go together!
Tweens will automatically reach for them, so always keep
some handy in the freezer. Replace the sugar-laden, calorie-
dense and artificially-coloured commercial versions with
this pure fruit lolly. Tangy, sweet and cool, these lollies will be
loved by every child.

White dragon fruit 1/4 (125 g / 4 1/4 oz)

Ripe yellow kiwi fruit 1 (150 g / 5 1/3 oz)

Ripe mango 1/4 (175 g / 6 1/2 oz)

Lemon juice 1 tsp

Low-fat yoghurt 1/2 cup (125 ml / 4 fl oz)

Sugar 1 Tbsp

Place all ingredients in a blender and blend until smooth.

Pour mixture into 8 popsicle moulds. Place in the freezer
overnight to set.

Unmould with care and serve immediately.

nutrition fact

Dragon fruit, a recent arrival in
the markets of Southeast Asia,
is the fruit of the cactus plant.
The brilliant pink skin conceals
a white or pink flesh which is
speckled with tiny black seeds.
Dragon fruit is rich in fluid,
vitamin C and fibre.

cooking tip

This recipe works with any
blend of fresh fruit, so go
ahead and create your own
lollies, using one or more
fruit of your tween's choice.
The fruit blend is delicious
enough to be served as a
refreshing smoothie.

4 pax

8 min

20 min

yummy yam dreams

The inspiration for this smooth, creamy dessert is the traditional 'or nee' — a fragrant yam paste that is high in fat, saturated fat and sugar. In our healthier version, we have coloured the yam a pale lavender using the leaves of the oyster plant (*tradescantia spathacea*), or 'bang hua' as it is known in Chinese (see Cooking Tip).

Yam 1 small (400 g / 14¹/₃ oz)
Water 3 cups (750 ml / 24 fl oz)
Oyster plant leaf 1, washed
Rock sugar 120 g (4¹/₄ oz)
Canned gingko nuts 16 nuts, drained

Peel yam and cut into large cubes.

Bring water to the boil in a large pot. Add yam cubes, oyster plant leaf and rock sugar, and cook until yam is soft.

Remove leaf and discard. Set aside 2 cubes of yam and leave to cool. Cut into small cubes.

Blend remaining yam with cooking liquid into a very smooth paste.

Spoon yam paste into 4 cups and top with yam cubes and gingko nuts. Serve warm.

Source: Manganese
Good Source: Vitamin C

Nutritional Analysis (per serving)

Energy 230 kcal   Saturated fat 0 g
Protein 2 g   Cholesterol 0 mg
Carbohydrate 57 g   Calcium 46 mg
Dietary fibre 4.1 g   Iron 1.1 mg
Total fat 0.2 g

4 pax

10 min

2 hr

pear paradise

Gently steaming the pear makes the flesh sweeter and softer. We have intensified the sweetness naturally, with red dates and dried longans

Chinese pears 2 large (600 g 1 lb 5^1/$_3$ oz), peeled, cored and halved

Red dates 65 g (2^1/$_3$ oz)

Dried longans 20 g (^{2}/$_3$ oz)

Rock sugar 20 g (^{2}/$_3$ oz)

Place Chinese pears on a steaming plate in a steamer, with the cut side facing up. Place red dates, dried longans and rock sugar into hollowed out centre of pears.

Cover steamer and steam ingredients for 2 hours.

Remove plate from steamer. Arrange pears in serving bowls and serve warm.

Brown rice pudding

A blend of Western and Eastern ingredients, this pudding is rich in fibre. It can be enjoyed as a sweet ending to a meal or as a healthy snack.

Light brown rice ¹/₃ cup (65 g / 2¹/₃ oz)

Red rice 2 Tbsp

Pearl barley 2 Tbsp

Low-fat evaporated milk ²/₃ cup (165 ml / 5¹/₂ fl oz)

Brown sugar 1 Tbsp

Raisins 1 Tbsp

Almond essence 1 tsp

Almond flakes 1 Tbsp

Garnish

Ripe persimmon 1 medium (170 g / 6 oz), finely chopped

Chopped palm sugar 2 tsp

Bring a large pot of water to the boil. Add brown and red rice and barley grains and boil until grains are tender. Drain.

Place cooked rice and barley mixture into a pressure cooker. Add evaporated milk, brown sugar and raisins. When steam rises, place the weight and cook for 10 more minutes. Leave mixture to cool before removing from pressure cooker.

Alternatively, place ingredients in a slow-cooker and cook until grains are soft and tender.

Add almond essence and almond flakes to rice mixture. Keep warm.

Place palm sugar in a small saucepan with a little water to dissolve sugar. Place over low heat and stir to dissolve. Set aside.

Serve one scoop of rice pudding with chopped persimmon. Drizzle with palm sugar syrup.

4 pax

10 min

20 min

nutrition fact
Almonds are a good source of vitamin E and heart-healthy monounsaturated fats.

Good Source: Manganese

Nutritional Analysis (per serving)

Energy 130 kcal

Protein 5 g

Carbohydrate 25 g

Dietary fibre 1.6 g

Total fat 1.3 g

Saturated fat 0.2 g

Cholesterol 2 mg

Calcium 124 mg

Iron 6.7 mg

cooking tip
If persimmon is not available when you want to prepare this dish, replace it with a soft sweet fruit in season such as strawberries or mangoes.

Dietary Reference Intake (DRI) for Tweens

Nutrients	4–8 years	9–13 years
Proximates		
Total Water (L/d)	1.7	2.4
CHO (g/d)	130	130
Total Fibre (g/d)	25	31
Fat (g/d)	ND	ND
Linoleic Acid (g/d)	10	12
Alpha-Linolenic Acid (g/d)	0.9	1.2
Protein (g/d)	19	34
Vitamins		
Vitamin A (mcg/d)	400	600
Vitamin C (mg/d)	25	45
Vitamin D (mcg/d)	5	5
Vitamin E (mg/d)	7	11
Vitamin K (mcg/d)	55	60
Thiamin (mg/d)	0.6	0.9
Riboflavin (mg/d)	0.6	0.9
Niacin (mg/d)	8	12
Vitamin B$_6$ (mg/d)	0.6	1
Folate (mcg/d)	200	300
Vitamin B$_{12}$ (mcg/d)	1.2	1.8
Pantothenic acid (mg/d)	3	4
Biotin (mcg/d)	12	20
Choline (mg/d)	250	375

Nutrients	4–8 years	9–13 years
Minerals		
Calcium (mg)	800	1300
Chromium (mcg)	15	25
Copper (mcg)	440	700
Fluoride (mg/d)	1	2
Iodine (mcg/d)	90	120
Iron (mg/d)	10	8
Magnesium (mg/d)	130	240
Manganese (mg/d)	1.5	1.9
Molybdenum (mcg/d)	22	34
Phosphorus (mg/d)	500	1250
Selenium (mcg/d)	30	40
Zinc (mg/d)	5	8
Potassium (g/d)	3.8	4.5
Sodium (g/d)	1.2	1.5
Chloride (g/d)	1.9	2.3

Source: Food and Nutrition Board, Institute of Medicine, National Academies

Additional Reading Material for Parents

Books and Pamphlets

Birth to Eighteen Years – Dietary Tips for Your Child's Wellbeing, Health Promotion Board, Singapore, November 2007. http://www.hpb.gov.sg/hpb/default.asp?pg_id=935

How to Get Kids to Eat Great, Dr Christine Wood, Griffin Publishing, 2006.

Yummy! Every Parent's Nutrition Bible, Jane Clarke, Hodder & Stoughton, 2006.

ABC Guide to Fit Kids. A Companion for Parents and Families, Phillip Mason et al. Murdoch Books Pty Limited, 2007.

Websites

Agri-Food and Veterinary Authority of Singapore http://www.ava.gov.sg/

American Academy of Pediatrics http://www.aap.org/

American Dietetic Association http://www.eatright.org/cps/rde/xchg/ada/hs.xsl/index.html

Asian Food Information Centre http://www.afic.org/

Better Health Channel http://www.betterhealth.vic.gov.au/

Center for Science in the Public Interest http://www.cspinet.org

Food Standards Agency http://www.food.gov.uk/healthiereating/

Fruits and Veggies More Matters http://www.fruitsandveggiesmorematters.org/

Health Promotion Board, Singapore http://www.hpb.gov.sg

International Food Information Council http://www.ific.org/

Medline Plus http://www.nlm.nih.gov/medlineplus/childnutrition.html

National Dairy Council http://www.nutritionexplorations.com/kids/kitchen-main.asp

References

Dietary Guidelines for Children and Adolescents for the Healthcare Professional, Health Promotion Board, Singapore, 2007.

Healthy Eating for Preteens and Teens, Leslie Beck, Penguin Group Ltd, 2005.

Hot Potatoes and Cool Bananas. Healthy Food — What, Why and How. Perera A, Lister, C and Hedges, L. SNP International Publishing, 2007.

Eat, Play and Be Healthy, W. Allan Walker, McGraw-Hill, 2005

Resources

NutriBase Clinical Nutrition Manager, v 7.17

Nutrient Data Laboratory, USDA National Nutrient Database for Standard Reference

Food Info Search, Health Promotion Board, Singapore

NutriWEB Malaysia, Malaysian Foods Composition Database

About the Authors

Anna Jacob is a nutritionist and dietitian with over 20 years of experience. She provides nutrition consulting services to individuals, nursing homes, food companies, food retailers, government and non-governmental bodies and schools, both within Singapore and the region. Anna is keenly sought after by clients for her writing, editorial and speaking skills.

Anna earned a bachelor's degree in Nutrition and Dietetics and master's degree in Food Service Management and Dietetics from the Women's Christian College, Madras, India. She is also a full member of the Singapore Nutrition and Dietetics Association (SNDA).

Her first book, *First Foods*, written with four other dietitians, is a bestseller.

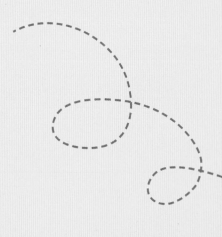

A nutritionist by training, Ng Hooi Lin provides nutrition consultancy services through the development of nutrition and health-focused workshops, as well as the facilitation of nutrition education programmes. Her aim is to make local nutrition information practical, accessible and personal, and she keeps a personal blog (http://nghooilin.blogspot.com) to support nutrition education among tech savvy Mandarin speakers. The Chinese language blog registers over 500 hits a day and has been positively reviewed by the Chinese newspapers in Singapore and Malaysia.

Hooi Lin is a full member of the Singapore Nutrition and Dietetic Association (SNDA).

Weights and Measures

Quantities for this book are given in Metric, Imperial and American (spoon and cup) measures. Standard spoon and cup measurements used are: *1 tsp = 5 ml, 1 Tbsp = 15 ml, 1 cup = 250 ml.* All measures are level unless otherwise stated.

Liquid and Volume Measures

Metric	Imperial	American
5 ml	1/6 fl oz	1 teaspoon
10 ml	1/3 fl oz	1 dessertspoon
15 ml	1/2 fl oz	1 tablespoon
60 ml	2 fl oz	1/4 cup (4 tablespoons)
85 ml	2 1/2 fl oz	1/3 cup
90 ml	3 fl oz	3/8 cup (6 tablespoons)
125 ml	4 fl oz	1/2 cup
180 ml	6 fl oz	3/4 cup
250 ml	8 fl oz	1 cup
300 ml	10 fl oz (1/2 pint)	1 1/4 cups
375 ml	12 fl oz	1 1/2 cups
435 ml	14 fl oz	1 3/4 cups
500 ml	16 fl oz	2 cups
625 ml	20 fl oz (1 pint)	2 1/2 cups
750 ml	24 fl oz (1 1/5 pints)	3 cups
1 litre	32 fl oz (1 3/5 pints)	4 cups
1.25 litres	40 fl oz (2 pints)	5 cups
1.5 litres	48 fl oz (2 2/5 pints)	6 cups
2.5 litres	80 fl oz (4 pints)	10 cups

Dry Measures

Metric	Imperial
30 grams	1 ounce
45 grams	1 1/2 ounces
55 grams	2 ounces
70 grams	2 1/2 ounces
85 grams	3 ounces
100 grams	3 1/2 ounces
110 grams	4 ounces
125 grams	4 1/2 ounces
140 grams	5 ounces
280 grams	10 ounces
450 grams	16 ounces (1 pound)
500 grams	1 pound, 1 1/2 ounces
700 grams	1 1/2 pounds
800 grams	1 3/4 pounds
1 kilogram	2 pounds, 3 ounces
1.5 kilograms	3 pounds, 4 1/2 ounces
2 kilograms	4 pounds, 6 ounces

Oven Temperature

	°C	°F	Gas Regulo
Very slow	120	250	1
Slow	150	300	2
Moderately slow	160	325	3
Moderate	180	350	4
Moderately hot	190/200	375/400	5/6
Hot	210/220	410/425	6/7
Very hot	230	450	8
Super hot	250/290	475/550	9/10

Length

Metric	Imperial
0.5 cm	1/4 inch
1 cm	1/2 inch
1.5 cm	3/4 inch
2.5 cm	1 inch

Abbreviation

tsp	teaspoon
Tbsp	tablespoon
g	gram
kg	kilogram
ml	millilitre